THE COMPLETE HOT SAUCE COOKBOOK

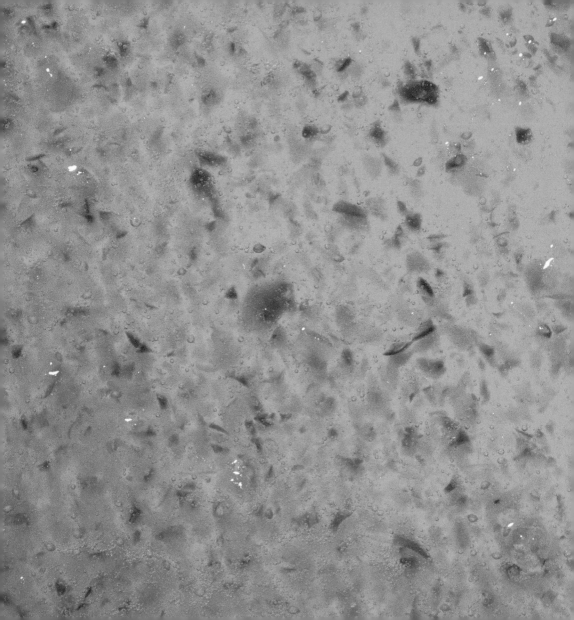

THE
complete
hot
sauce
COOKBOOK

60 Fiery Hot Sauce Recipes from Around the World

MICHAEL VALENCIA

Photography by Paul Sirisalee

ROCKRIDGE
PRESS

For general information on our other products and services or to obtain technical support, please contact our Customer Care Department within the United States at (866) 744-2665, or outside the United States at (510) 253-0500.

Rockridge Press publishes its books in a variety of electronic and print formats. Some content that appears in print may not be available in electronic books, and vice versa.

Interior and Cover Designer: Antonio Valverde
Art Producer: Michael Hardgrove
Editor: Marjorie DeWitt
Production Editor: Emily Sheehan

Photography © 2020 Paul Sirisalee. Food Styling by Kimberley Sirisalee. All other images used under license from iStockphoto.com and Shutterstock.com.

ISBN: Print 978-1-64739-136-2 | eBook 978-1-64739-137-9
R0

TO MY FAMILY AND FRIENDS
WHO'VE BEEN THERE
FOR ME THROUGH EVERY STEP
OF THIS SPICY JOURNEY.
I LOVE YOU ALL. KEEP IT SPICY!

contents

Chapter Seven: Asia 85

Chapter Eight: Around the World 97

Chapter Nine: Other Hot Sauces 109

introduction

At 13 years old I remember picking fresh vegetables and peppers from a garden I grew in my parents' backyard. I was always the one they called on when they wanted a fresh batch of tasty salsa for dinner. This is when I discovered my love for hot sauces and spicy foods. Born in sunny Southern California and raised on the island of Kauai, Hawaii, I knew that I wanted to own a business someday and work for myself. I was always taught that with hard work, dedication, and proper planning, any dream can become a reality. Fast-forward 30 years and who would've known that I'd be living my dream. I now own and operate Mikey V's Foods LLC.

It all started professionally for me when my brother Marc dared me to enter my infamous salsa into the 2012 *Austin Chronicle* Hot Sauce Festival's annual contest. I won first place in the red sauce category out of hundreds of entrants. After that festival and much to my surprise, several retailers were asking for my salsa for their shelves. I was beyond ecstatic! There was just one problem: I didn't know how to get it bottled professionally. After thousands of hours of research, I finally got my salsa on the shelf of my first retail location. That all seemed like it happened decades ago. Since then, Mikey V's Foods has acquired four companies and has won over 200 awards in the spicy food and hot sauce industry.

The goal of this book is to share my passion for hot sauce, including its origins, and to give you a deep and comprehensive look into the world of hot sauce. We will be diving into several dozen recipes, including several techniques on how to make your own hot sauce unique and flavorful.

CHAPTER ONE:

Hot Sauce 101

Hot sauce is a way of life for me. I can't go one meal without adding the flavors and heat of my bottled obsessions. You will even catch me bringing my favorite hot sauce into a restaurant with me. Hot sauce has gained popularity throughout the years and is becoming a staple in almost every household and restaurant. Today there are thousands of hot sauces available commercially. Early pioneers of hot sauces include Tabasco Brand Pepper Sauce (one of my favorites), which paved the way for other companies to open their doors and help create this vast niche market. Follow me as we learn everything there is to know about hot sauce!

What Is a Hot Sauce?

Hot sauces are the most popular and widely used condiment in the world. They are most commonly used to add additional flavor and spice to a meal. Most true hot sauces have one common ingredient: a chile pepper. Adding vinegar and a combination of fruits and vegetables provides the base of a regular hot sauce recipe. Hot sauces come in different forms: liquid, salsas (chunky), and powders.

A HISTORY OF HOT SAUCE

It is unclear how long hot sauce has been around, but it's believed that ancient Mayan civilizations grew chile peppers for thousands of years. They would grind a combination of chile peppers, tomatoes, onions, and garlic in a mortar and pestle called a molcajete. This paste or salsa would then be added to their food for flavor and spice. Men, women, and children enjoyed these spicy concoctions.

In the late 1400s, the Spanish found different varieties of chile peppers while traveling through the Caribbean and South and Central America. They traded these capsaicin-filled peppers all over the world.

In 1868, hot sauce started being mass-produced in America. A man by the name of Edmund McIlhenny, the founder of Tabasco brand products, decided that the food in Louisiana was too bland.

Using the Tabasco chile peppers grown on his own Avery Island, he created a pepper sauce to add more flavor and spice. He sold over 650 bottles to grocers in America and Europe. Today, Tabasco is the most recognized and most popular hot sauce in the world. It's sold in over 195 countries and territories.

According to *The Atlantic*, in the 1990s hot sauce and salsa overtook ketchup as America's number one condiment. They remain more popular than ever.

WHY DO WE LOVE HOT SAUCES SO MUCH?

Let's face it. Hot sauce is not only tasty but addicting! Its appeal has caught the curiosity of brave souls who challenge themselves—or others—to taste the hottest sauces out there. Grocery chains are now dedicating aisles in their stores to artisanal and mass-produced hot sauces and salsas. There are challenges on social media to eat the hottest-rated pepper or sauce or candy. YouTube shows like First We Feast's *Hot Ones* contribute to making hot sauce more popular. The premise of the *Hot Ones* show is simple: Celebrities go on the show to promote their new movie, album, book, or whatever. While being interviewed by host Sean Evans, they are challenged to eat a plate of hot wings drenched in hot sauces from mild to extra hot. Their egos—and spice levels—are tested on camera for the world to see.

In addition to pepper-eating challenges on social media, there are currently over 60 festivals around the globe that focus on spicy foods and hot sauce. Attendees can walk around and sample each spicy food manufacturer's products while sipping on a cold beverage and listening to a local band. The *Austin Chronicle* Hot Sauce Festival is one of the longest-running shows in operation. The show opened its doors in 1990 as a small hot sauce contest and has grown into one of the largest hot sauce festivals around. Held in late August, the festival attracts more than 10,000 people and 350 entrants to its contests. Small hot sauce and spicy food manufacturers use this festival as the launching pad for their businesses. That's exactly how my company, Mikey V's Foods, got its start.

Hot sauces and spicy food are now a huge business. Hot sauce stores are now popping up in almost every town. Chain restaurants are even getting in on the spicy food sensation. Jack in the Box has a sriracha cheeseburger, and Taco Bell offers the Doritos Locos Taco. For a limited time, Popeyes restaurants even offered ghost pepper chicken wings!

Farmers and horticulturalists are constantly crossbreeding peppers in the hopes of being the first to discover the hottest all-natural pepper for Guinness World Records, which currently classifies the Carolina Reaper as the world's hottest pepper.

CAPTIVATING CAPSAICIN

Capsaicin is the component found in chile peppers that causes the burning sensation usually felt when eating spicy foods. Spicy peppers are commonly used in hot sauces and are the number one ingredient in making a sauce spicy. Ingesting capsaicin in any form tricks the brain into thinking your mouth is on fire. Your body then produces endorphins to help extinguish that bad sensation your body is feeling. The result is the endorphin rush or "high" you get when eating spicy foods.

WHY YOU SHOULD MAKE YOUR OWN

Taste is extremely subjective. I like hot; you like mild. I like sweet; you like salty. Hot sauce can be a fun way to experiment in the kitchen, creating your very own spicy concoction that's personalized to your taste buds.

Many commercial manufacturers still use chemical preservatives like sodium benzoate to help extend the shelf life of acidic foods. Many believe that these types of harmful chemical preservatives are linked to cancer. We live in a health-conscious society that wants to use more natural preservatives instead of chemical ones. Making your own sauce guarantees that the ingredients you use are all natural, and the best part is that you're using fresh ingredients each time.

Making your own hot sauce can save you a few bucks, too. Once you get your recipe right, you will find that it is more cost-effective to make your own. Hot sauce making requires a lot of patience. You can't just snap your fingers and, *voilà*, have the perfect sauce. You need to put some thought into it. Pairing the right sauce with the right dish is key.

Types of Hot Sauces

Hot sauces come in many forms: thin ones, thick ones, spicy ones, mild ones, red ones, green ones. There are two classifications for hot sauces: blended, which is referred to as a hot sauce, and unblended, which is recognized as a salsa. The ingredients are sometimes the same; the consistency and applications are what separate these two condiments. I happen to love both!

BLENDED

A traditional-style hot sauce is finely blended. It is sometimes strained so that very little pulp is left. Blended hot sauces are more concentrated in heat than the unblended form. They are used to spice up food and soups and are sometimes used as a marinade. Tabasco, Tapatío, and Cholula sauces are examples of finely blended sauces that are used to add flavor to dishes. A salsa can also be blended and is known as a "cantina" style salsa.

UNBLENDED

Salsa, which is Spanish for "sauce," is most popular in the United States and Mexico. It is basically all the ingredients of a hot sauce, slightly blended to leave a chunky texture. It is traditional for Mexican restaurants to serve chips and salsa as an appetizer prior to the main dish. It is probably the most popular appetizer, as one can get carried away with a bowl of chips and a good fresh salsa. Salsas can be cooked or served raw. Pico de gallo salsas and the African peri-peri sauce are examples of unblended, fresh sauces.

REGIONAL STYLES

We eat foods according to our culinary traditions. We connect to our culture and ethnic groups through food, and the same goes for hot sauces. There are many regionally based flavor profiles to choose from. Fresh peppers that were once native to a region have acclimated to the weather elsewhere and are now grown in different climates. For example, the Bhut Jolokia pepper, also known as the "ghost pepper," originated in India and is now grown widely in the United States and other parts of the world.

North America

There are several styles of hot sauces in North America, including common Mexican hot sauces and salsas. Two other popular choices are Louisiana- and New Mexico-style sauces. The most commonly used peppers across these types are cayenne, Hatch, jalapeño, chipotle, and habanero. All sauces use similar ingredients: vinegar and salt with the pepper of your choice for heat.

Louisiana sauces typically contain only a few ingredients: vinegar, cayenne pepper, salt, and garlic. Most Louisiana-style sauces are aged for a minimum of 30 days to give the flavors a chance to come together. Using a higher volume of vinegar and a cayenne pepper as a base is what classifies a sauce as "Louisiana." Hawaiian chile pepper water is considered a Louisiana style of sauce because of its high vinegar content—it's really more like a spicy seasoned vinegar. It is customary to use authentic red chile peppers grown only in Hawaii for this sauce. Fresh garlic, water, and Hawaiian sea salt finish off this five-ingredient recipe.

Green chiles are known to have originated in New Mexico. When roasted over an open flame, these peppers are used in a sauce and added to dishes. Just about every restaurant in New Mexico offers green and red chile options with its pork, chicken, or beef dishes. Hatch green chiles from New Mexico are harvested, roasted, and then sold in late summer and early autumn.

Also gaining popularity in North America are the "super-hot" peppers—all peppers hotter than a habanero are classified as super-hots.

South America and Central America

Aji picante and guasacaca sauces seem to rule the palates of South Americans, especially when eaten with empanadas and plantains. Similar to New Mexico's red and green options, there seems to be a strong divide between Colombia and Venezuela when it comes to these sauces. Aji picante contains red chiles and sometimes tomatoes and is used primarily by the Colombians. Guasacaca is referred to as "Venezuelan guacamole" and contains bell pepper, avocado, cilantro, and parsley. Regardless of the type of food that is being eaten, you can bet there will be either one of these sauces on it.

Caribbean

Hot sauce is commonly known as pepper sauce in the Caribbean. They use a variety of extra-hot peppers, including the Scotch bonnet, habanero, Scorpion, and cayenne peppers. Garlic, salt, vinegar, and mustard are also used in Caribbean-style sauces. It's fairly common to incorporate tropical fruits native to the islands, such as mangos, papaya, and pineapple, into hot sauce recipes. Hot sauces that stem from this region are known to have intense heat. What many people would normally consider hot is mild in this region.

Asia

Similar to the hot sauces of North America, Asian-style sauces are regionally diverse. What these sauces have in common is garlic. It seems most of the sauces, no matter where in Asia they originate, contain garlic.

Gochujang is a staple of Korea. Traditionally this paste is made with red chiles, rice powder, fermented soy beans, and salt. It is used as a marinade in the ever-so-popular bulgogi beef dishes, stirred into dipping sauces, and added to soups.

The hot sauce used by most households in the Philippines is a hot banana sauce. It is made with bananas, garlic, onions, and a variety of spices. It's a thick and chunky sauce with a slow burn and is commonly used to season chicken and beef.

The Chinese often like to use a hot chile oil as their sauce. A soybean-based oil is added to red pepper flakes with the addition of garlic, salt, and a touch of sesame oil. A favorite in our household, this sauce is great in just about everything. It's most commonly used as a stir-fry base and an eggroll-dipping sauce.

Last but not least is one of the most popular hot sauces in the world, which was created in Vietnam. Sriracha, also known as "rooster sauce," graces the tables of just about every Asian restaurant in the United States. The sauce's creator, David Tran, immigrated to the United States in 1978 and brought with him a unique condiment made with red chile peppers, garlic, vinegar, and sugar. Currently, this sauce remains the most popular hot sauce in the United States.

Other Regions

Just like North and South America, other regions such as Europe, Africa, and the Middle East have their own way of spicing up dishes. They make a fresh sauce daily or weekly that is generally uncooked. Compare it to making a fresh pico de gallo for your meals. Here are some well-known sauces that come from these countries.

Africa is known for its peri-peri or piri-piri sauce. This sauce is oil based and normally not cooked but served like a fresh salsa. The ingredients include a pound of African bird's eye chiles, fresh garlic, paprika, cilantro, basil, lemon juice, and salt. This sauce is a spicier sauce when the authentic bird's eye pepper is used, as opposed to the traditional jalapeño pepper that Americans are accustomed to.

Hungary has embraced paprika as its national spice. Hungarians create mild and spicy paprika paste that, when mixed with tomatoes, is used with dishes such as goulash and stews.

In the Middle East, harissa is a spicy paste made with roasted red peppers, serrano peppers, herbs, and spices. There are many recipes for the paste, varying from household to region. It is used to spice up dishes like couscous, soups, and stews and is even used as a meat marinade.

Shatta is a Middle Eastern hot sauce that is extremely popular in Egypt and Palestine. It is often used on koshari, a delicious and popular Egyptian rice dish. There are two variations of shatta—red and green. The difference between the two has to do with the amount of fresh green herbs used in the recipe. The green sauce has about five times as many herbs as its red counterpart.

CHAPTER TWO:

The Components of Hot Sauce

My first attempts at making hot sauce went like this: I started off by picking the vegetables and peppers from my garden. Like a novice, I would blend them together with some spices and vinegar until the result was palatable. Then I would add more hot peppers until the heat was just right. Now that I make hot sauce for a living, I can tell you there is much more to making a good sauce than I first thought.

What Goes into a Hot Sauce?

There are many different ingredients that can go into hot sauces: tomatoes, onions, garlic, salt, chile peppers, vinegar, and lime or lemon juice. Some even get creative by adding fruits, juices, alcohol, and exotic flavors like truffle oil. What I have found is that most hot sauces have several common ingredients, no matter what region they come from. Acids exist in nearly all hot sauces, and magic is found in the additional flavorings that make each sauce special and unique. When it comes to making a hot sauce though, the single most important ingredient is the chile pepper. What is a hot sauce without any heat?

Peppers

Capsicum fruits, otherwise known as chile peppers, got their name from Christopher Columbus as he returned from a trip. It was said that he sampled a chile pepper and said it had the spice of black pepper, thus naming it a "pepper." There are several variants of peppers ranging in heat from mild to "melt your face off." Choosing the right pepper for the right hot sauce is a crucial element when creating it. Will you use a fresh pod? Mash? Dried peppers? Powders?

FRESH PEPPERS AND MASH

I feel like a kid at Disneyland every time I go to the grocery store and gather my ingredients for my next hot sauce. I like to handpick each item, knowing that when I'm finished I'll have a masterpiece. Since chile peppers have become mainstream, it is easy to find common peppers like jalapeño, serrano, and habanero peppers in your local grocery store year-round.

Jalapeño peppers are the most common of the three. These are the most popular pepper in North America as well as the mildest. They are normally picked and used while still green but are also eaten when the peppers have ripened to a deep red color. Jalapeños are most often used in fresh salsas and hot sauces.

Serrano peppers are also eaten when green or red. These peppers are a bit smaller and spicier than the jalapeño. They are in the spicy heat range of 8,000 to 18,000 Scoville Heat Units (SHU), whereas jalapeños are 2,500 to 4,000 SHU. Serrano peppers are generally used in making pico de gallo and salsa.

Habanero peppers are the spiciest of these peppers. They range in heat from 100,000 to 350,000 SHU. These peppers are thin walled and have a waxy appearance. Habanero peppers are used when orange or red, but recently growers have crossbred these peppers for coloring purposes. Now we can find green, yellow, brown, and purple variations. These peppers are used in making a very spicy hot sauce or salsa.

A mash is another way to introduce fresh peppers to hot sauces or salsas but in a more concentrated form. Mashes are made by grinding these fresh peppers and adding a small amount of vinegar for preservation. I like to use mashes in some of my "super-hot" salsas.

DRIED PEPPERS AND POWDERS

After a good harvest of fresh peppers, sometimes you will have an abundance of peppers that cannot be used immediately. Instead of tossing those peppers out, why not dehydrate them for use year-round? This is common practice for super-hot peppers that are harvested only once a year. Some dried peppers are ground up and turned into powders. The use of dried peppers and powders has been around for years. Dried ancho, árbol, guajillo, and pequin peppers are found in most grocery stores. These peppers are on the milder side and are used to add heat and texture in sauces like mole or enchilada sauce. I sometimes use powders and dried peppers in my recipes because it brings a different element of heat to my concoctions. Powders are a bit milder than the fresh pepper but make the heat linger for a longer period.

THE SCOVILLE SCALE

An American pharmacist by the name of Wilbur Scoville created the Scoville scale, which measures the heat from chile peppers and other spicy foods. He developed his Scoville Heat Unit (SHU) in 1912, based on the concentrated number of capsaicinoids, the compounds in which capsaicin is present. This is the most commonly used form of measuring chile heat today. Some will argue that this is an unscientific measurement because of the human subjectivity in how individuals handle spice. In other words, if you and I ate the same jalapeño pepper, you might think it is far spicier than I do, since I have a higher tolerance for heat. A more scientific method is being developed called high-performance liquid chromatography (HPLC). This method measures capsaicin and its concentrated pungency. The bell pepper has the lowest amount of heat on the Scoville scale (0 SHU), whereas the Carolina Reaper is at the top at a whopping 1.4 million SHU.

15 peppers

Bell peppers: 0 SHU

Anaheim pepper: 500–2,500 SHU

Poblano pepper: 1,000–1,500 SHU

Hungarian pepper: 2,000–8,000 SHU

Jalapeño pepper: 2,500–4,000 SHU

Serrano pepper: 8,000–18,000 SHU

Tabasco pepper: 30,000–50,000 SHU

Cayenne pepper: 35,000–60,000 SHU

The Complete Hot Sauce Cookbook

mild to hottest

Red Thai pepper: 50,000–100,000 SHU

Scotch bonnet pepper: 100,000–325,000 SHU

Habanero peppers: 100,000–350,000 SHU

Fatalii peppers: 125,000–375,000 SHU

Ghost pepper: 850,000–1,000,000 SHU

Trinidad Scorpion pepper: 1,200,000–2,000,000 SHU

Carolina Reaper pepper: 1,400,000–2,200,000 SHU

Acids

Acids are commonly used in most hot sauces for a couple of reasons. The first reason is that acid is used to provide "tart-like" flavoring to the sauce. This sharp flavor is usually added in the form of vinegar, citric acid crystals, or citric juices. The second reason is that these acids provide some defense against oxidation and microbial growth. *Ewww*! By using acids and an approved bottling process, you can make your hot sauce shelf-stable, which means you don't have to refrigerate it until you open it.

VINEGARS

Vinegars are the most popular acids to use when making hot sauces. There are dozens of types of vinegars you can use. The most common to use in hot sauces is white vinegar. White vinegar comes in different strengths, and the percentage of acidity determines how strong in flavor any vinegar is. Apple cider vinegar is another vinegar used in hot sauces; it provides a more tart flavor and is much milder than traditional white vinegar. I like to use exotic flavors like black, yuzu, pineapple, and coconut vinegars, especially when making a tropical-style hot sauce. They'll be sure to give you the excitement you're looking for.

OTHERS

Citric acid and fruit juices are another way to achieve the same goals of maintaining acidity levels without the addition of sharp-tasting vinegars. Adding lime or lemon juice or citric acid crystals gives your sauce different flavors and can help you customize your sauce however you like.

HOTTER THAN HABANEROS

If you've been eating hot sauce and salsa for as long as I have, you know that you gain a tolerance for spicy foods. After starting with a mild jalapeño-based sauce or a cayenne sauce such as Frank's RedHot, you'll find yourself gradually wanting a hotter version as time goes by. Luckily, farmers and horticulturalists are listening to our pleas. As we speak, there are people creating new crossbred peppers that go way above and beyond the heat of the habanero pepper. Some hotter peppers that you can currently find on the market today include:

* **Scotch bonnet:** 100,000–325,000 SHU
* **Fatalii pepper:** 350,000–500,000 SHU
* **Bhut Jolokia (ghost pepper):** 850,000–1,000,000 SHU
* **Trinidad Scorpion:** 1,200,000–2,000,000 SHU
* **Carolina Reaper:** 1,400,000–2,200,000 SHU

Other Flavorings

Using other flavors is just as important as the chile pepper you choose to make a hot sauce spicy. Things like spices and fruits help make it tasty (or tastier!). The use of these ingredients brings depth to your sauce, which is very important. Who wants a sauce just for heat and not flavor? Adding spices such as coriander, black pepper, and garlic powder will bring an added touch to your sauce. Salts such as kosher salt, garlic salt, and sea salt bring a much-needed component to your hot sauce, turning it from bland to zesty. Using fruits and vegetables will bring an additional level of complexity to your sauce that is sure to please many palates. I think ginger, garlic, and onions are musts when creating all sauces.

CHAPTER THREE:

Making Your Own Hot Sauce

This is the chapter you have been waiting for! You get to make your own hot sauce! In this chapter, you're going to learn some techniques and tricks to help you create your hot sauce masterpiece. We'll also dig into preservation, bottling, and even what to do when your mouth is on fire after eating a spicy sauce or hot pepper.

Equipment

Here is a list of essential equipment you will need when making your first batch of hot sauce:

Nonreactive pot: A nonreactive pot is a pot or pan that, like the name suggests, does not react to acidic foods like hot sauces and salsas. The reason for using a nonreactive pot is that these types of pots won't impart a metallic flavor or change the color of your hot sauces when you use them. A few examples of nonreactive materials are stainless steel, ceramic, glass, and metal cookware with an enamel coating. Steer clear of reactive pots and pans like aluminum and cast iron when making a hot sauce.

Mixing spoon: I use my lucky green mixing spoon when I make a batch of hot sauce. I think it's more like a rubber spatula. This helps me when I'm scraping the sides of my blender carafe, ensuring I get all the sauce off the sides.

High-speed blender or food processor: There are several commercial blenders and food processors to choose from. I like my Vitamix blender and Cuisinart food processor. Whatever you choose, sticking with equipment helps you achieve consistency when you remake your sauce.

Glass hot sauce bottles: Glass bottles are used instead of plastic in most cases because they are nonreactive. When adding an acidic product to a plastic bottle, hot sauces will eat away at the plastic bottle over time. Glass bottles maintain freshness and flavor better than plastic bottles do, which is why pickles, beer, and wine are bottled in glass.

Foam-lined lids: Foam-lined caps have the preferred liner for bottling because they have a low moisture transmission rate (meaning they seldom leak) as well as taste and odor resistance.

A funnel (one that fits in your bottles!): It's important to get a funnel that fits your bottle snugly because pressure can build inside your bottle when pouring hot liquids, something that will happen when hot filling your bottles (see page 36). You always want to be very careful when filling your bottles.

Ladle or scoop: Sometimes you need a special ladle when filling bottles, especially if your sauce is on the thicker side. Most of the time you will use a scoop or small pitcher.

Mask or goggles: Besides the fact that you are cooking a hot sauce that is going to be boiling hot, you are also handling spicy peppers. Eye protection is a must! Trust me on this one!

A well-ventilated kitchen: Open your windows and turn your fans on! Spicy ingredients tend to get even spicier when you cook them. Years ago, I cleared my house out because I was sautéing Scorpion peppers for a salsa. My wife and kids were coughing and struggling to breathe. Oops! I didn't let that happen again.

FIERY FERMENTATION

Fermentation is one of the oldest methods of preserving foods. For years, people have fermented cheeses, wines, and vegetables. In the process of fermentation, we create an oxygen-free environment in which good bacteria can grow while harmful bacteria cannot survive. During this process, acids created by the good bacteria help preserve the food. By using the fermentation method when making hot sauce, you create a deeper, more pleasant taste. Peppers become milder and have a different texture.

A Starter Recipe

A question I get asked often is how I came up with certain recipes. The answer is I like to create a sauce based on what I'm cooking for dinner. Pairing a sauce with the main course is very important to me. Your sauce shouldn't overpower your food but complement it. (Unless my mother-in-law is cooking—then I want it to cover up that taste! Just kidding, Esther.) Here is a basic starter recipe you can use for your first hot sauce. Remember that there is no right or wrong way to make your hot sauce. Be creative! Try roasting your peppers or vegetables for a unique flavor.

BASIC HOT SAUCE

This recipe is the most fundamental recipe you can use to make a hot sauce. I use it as a base and substitute hotter peppers for spicier recipes.

Makes: 3 cups
Prep time:
10 minutes
Cook time:
15 minutes

18 TO 20 CHOPPED PEPPERS (SUCH AS CAYENNE, FRESNO, OR JALAPEÑO PEPPERS)

2 CUPS WHITE VINEGAR

1 TEASPOON KOSHER SALT, PLUS MORE TO TASTE

3 GARLIC CLOVES, ROUGHLY CHOPPED

1 In a large saucepan, combine the peppers, vinegar, salt, and garlic.

2 Bring to a boil over medium heat to soften the peppers, about 10 minutes.

3 Transfer the contents of the saucepan to a high-speed blender or food processor and puree.

4 Taste and add salt, as desired.

5 Bottle in a glass container with a foam-lined cap (see page 29).

6 Store in the refrigerator for up to 3 weeks.

Ingredient Tip: Roast peppers prior to cooking them for a great roasted sauce. You can also switch out the white vinegar for apple cider vinegar for a sweeter flavor.

SAFETY FIRST!

While you might think it's cool to chop up a pound of Carolina Reaper peppers with your bare hands, you can cause yourself some major discomfort and skin irritation by doing so. Here are some helpful tips when you making your own hot sauce:

* Always wear gloves when handling hot peppers.
* Wear eye protection while chopping peppers and making hot sauce.
* Use a well-ventilated kitchen with a fan while cooking hot sauce.
* Wash all utensils such as knives and cutting boards that come in contact with hot peppers.
* Cool ingredients before blending. The steam will build up pressure and pop the top of the blender if you're not careful.

MY MOUTH'S ON FIRE!

We've all been there before: sitting down at a Mexican restaurant and digging into the fresh bowl of chips and salsa when BAM!, the capsaicin hits your mouth and tongue like you just took a bite out of the sun! Beads of sweat start to form above your lip and brows. You take a drink of water, and it doesn't seem to help. What to do now? How do you get this burning sensation out of your mouth? Here are four remedies for cooling off your tongue in dire situations:

1 **Milk:** Sipping milk seems to be the most effective remedy for putting out the fire in your mouth. A protein found in milk called casein helps break the bond that capsaicin forms on the nerve receptors on your tongue.

2 **Sugar or honey:** A sugar packet or teaspoon of honey will temporarily slow down the burning sensation in your mouth. The sugar absorbs the spicy capsaicin oil.

3 **Chocolate:** Eating a chocolate bar is another way for some temporary mouth-burning relief, especially milk chocolate. Like milk, the casein in the chocolate bar breaks that bond and allows for much-needed relief. Dark chocolate works as well, but I don't think it works as fast.

4 **Bread:** Eating bread is another effective way to soothe your tongue. The bread soaks up the capsaicin oils and reduces the burn fast and effectively.

Preserving Your Hot Sauces

The acidity of a sauce is the main factor in how long your sauce will keep. When it comes to preserving your hot sauce, there are a couple of things you must know. First, your sauce needs to have some form of natural acid added to it to protect it from bacterial growth. Vinegars, citric acid, salt, and lemon or lime juices are several common ingredients used for this purpose. The more vinegar you add, the lower the pH will be. The second important thing to know is that you must have a cooking and bottling process.

PRESERVING WHEN BOTTLING

In order to obtain a shelf life for your hot sauce, you must use a special process when cooking and bottling. It is very important to measure your pH levels 24 to 48 hours after your sauce has hit its full equilibrium (when your sauce reaches its stable pH). A pH meter, easily found on Amazon, will help you measure this. The target pH for a novice sauce maker is 4.2. I like to see sauces under 4.0. Use the following steps to help you with your cooking and bottling process.

1. Wash all vegetables.
2. Put the ingredients in a high-speed blender, including acids (vinegar or lime or lemon juice).
3. Transfer the puree to a pot and bring to a boil, stirring constantly.

4. Lower the heat and simmer for 30 minutes.
5. Bottle at no less than 180°F.
6. Wipe the rim of the bottle and immediately cap it.
7. Invert the bottle for 3 minutes.

When you use this bottling method and a recipe that contains at least 20 percent vinegar, you should have nothing to worry about. Remember to check your pH levels after each batch.

PRESERVING AFTER OPENING

I often get asked if a hot sauce should be stored in the refrigerator after it has been opened. My answer has two parts. I typically do not store commercially made hot sauces in the refrigerator. However, I do store homemade sauces in the refrigerator. The reason for not refrigerating the commercially made sauces is because the ratio of vinegar to other ingredients in a commercial hot sauce is in perfect balance and bacteria will not grow in it.

Here are a few things you can do to help preserve the sauces you make or buy after opening the bottle:

* Sterilize your bottles by washing with hot water and submerging in a sanitizing solution.
* Keep the tip of the bottle and cap free of food and debris when storing it.
* Make sure your refrigerator is at least as low as 49°F.
* Add some natural preservatives such as vinegar, lime juice, or citric acid to your recipe.

7 Tips for Making a Great Hot Sauce

1. Always use the freshest, highest-quality ingredients.
2. Layer your sauces. Use a base such as tomatoes or tomatillos. Use an aromatic flavor like garlic, ginger, or onion. Use a vegetable or fruit when choosing a flavor profile (roasted bell pepper, onion, carrot, etc.). Do you want it sweet? Savory? A combination of both? Use a pepper like jalapeño, habanero, or ghost pepper when choosing your spice level. Finally, choose a natural preservative such as vinegar, lime juice, or citric acid.
3. Add a natural thickener like xanthan gum to thicken your hot sauces.
4. Add a ground powder or capsaicin extract to your hot sauce to make it spicier without changing the consistency.
5. Add fruits, fruit juices, sugar, or honey to make a sauce sweeter.

6. Blend, cook, and then bottle. That's how I like to make my sauces. Some people prefer cooking before blending, which is okay, but I find it's easier to bottle directly after cooking and not have to reheat (as you would if you blend second).

7. Use different vinegars for different flavor profiles. There are several dozen vinegars to choose from. The vinegars most used for making hot sauces are white and apple cider vinegars. I like using a combination of both. Sometimes I use a flavored vinegar depending on the sauce I'm creating—a Japanese yuzu vinegar is a great way to add a citrus flavor to your sauce.

the spice rating

The recipes in this book will contain a spice rating from 1 to 5 peppers (1 pepper being a mild sauce to 5 peppers being a tongue scorcher). With taste and heat levels being so subjective, this rating is based on the average person's idea of "spicy."

 Mild (like jalapeño or poblano peppers)

 Medium (like serrano peppers)

 Hot (like habanero peppers)

 X Hot (like ghost peppers)

 Melt Your Face Off
(like Scorpion peppers or the feared Carolina Reaper)

CHAPTER FOUR:

North America

Here in North America we have the most diverse styles of hot sauces. America has become a settling ground for many immigrants who have brought with them their unique culinary culture. Many Americans have grown accustomed to this vast array of foods and have created sauces that pair with them. After using some of these adopted recipes and adding American-grown super-spicy peppers, it's no wonder hot sauce became ingrained in the culture of America.

AUTHENTIC RESTAURANT-STYLE RED SALSA

This is the most common recipe that people ask me for, since it's one of my favorites. It is an authentic, home-cooked version of the salsa served at many Mexican restaurants. Now you can fine dine in the comfort of your home.

Makes: 2 quarts
Prep time: 10 minutes
Cook time: 10 minutes

5 ROMA TOMATOES, HALVED
1 SMALL WHITE ONION, HALVED
4 WHOLE GARLIC CLOVES
2 JALAPEÑO PEPPERS, HALVED
1 SERRANO PEPPER, HALVED
2 DRIED CHILE DE ARBOL PEPPERS
2 TABLESPOONS EXTRA-VIRGIN OLIVE OIL
½ CUP CHOPPED FRESH CILANTRO
¼ CUP FRESHLY SQUEEZED LIME JUICE
SALT
FRESHLY GROUND BLACK PEPPER

1 Put the tomatoes, the onion, the garlic, and all of the peppers on a flat pan on the stovetop.

2 Cook over medium-high heat until charred.

3 Remove from the heat and cool.

4 Put the contents of the flat pan in the bowl of a food processor.

5 Add the olive oil, cilantro, and lime juice and pulse until the sauce reaches the desired consistency. Add salt and pepper to taste.

6 Store in a sealed container in the refrigerator for up to 1 week.

Serving Tip: This sauce is best served immediately and is especially great with tortilla chips.

CHIPOTLE HOT SAUCE

This is without a doubt my favorite chipotle pepper hot sauce recipe. Smoky and aromatic, this sauce is great on meats and fabulous in stews and chilis.

Makes: 1 quart
Prep time: 5 minutes
Cook time:
20 minutes

2 MEDIUM-SIZE TOMATOES, DICED

½ MEDIUM WHITE ONION, DICED

1 (17-OUNCE) CAN CHIPOTLE PEPPERS IN ADOBO SAUCE

1 CUP WHITE VINEGAR

SALT

1 In a small saucepan, bring the tomatoes, onion, peppers, vinegar, and salt to a boil over medium heat.

2 Reduce the heat and simmer for 15 minutes. Add a splash of water if it gets too dry.

3 Remove from the heat and cool.

4 Transfer the mixture to a high-speed blender or food processor, and blend until it reaches the desired consistency. Salt to taste.

5 Put the sauce in sterilized bottles.

6 Store in the refrigerator for up to 3 months.

Ingredient Tip: Add water to the finished sauce if it is too thick.

LOUISIANA-STYLE HOT SAUCE

If you are like me and go out to eat often, there is a good chance you will see a bottle of Tabasco on the table of the restaurant you choose. Tabasco sauce is the world's most popular hot sauce—and for good reason. It is delicious and goes with almost everything. Now you can make your own Louisiana-style hot sauce!

Makes: about 2½ cups
Prep time: 30 minutes
Cook time: 25 minutes

5 CUPS CAYENNE PEPPERS, DICED
20 TO 25 GARLIC CLOVES, DICED
2 CUPS WHITE WINE VINEGAR
4 TEASPOONS KOSHER SALT, PLUS MORE TO TASTE

1. In a nonreactive medium saucepan, combine the peppers, garlic, vinegar, and salt and bring to a boil over medium heat.

2. Reduce the heat and simmer for 20 minutes, stirring occasionally. Remove from the heat and let cool.

3. Add the contents of the pot to a high-speed blender and puree.

4. Add additional salt to taste. Blend again, if necessary, to make the contents even easier to strain.

5. Strain the contents through a fine-mesh sieve or cheesecloth into a glass container.

6. Pour the liquid into sterilized hot sauce–style bottles.

7. Store in hot sauce-style bottles or another sealed container and refrigerate for up to 6 months.

Ingredient Tip: If you prefer a thicker sauce, do not strain.

ROASTED SALSA VERDE

This authentic Mexican recipe came from relatives who have been making it for years and is a favorite in my household. Try serving it as salsa with chips or use it on your favorite Mexican dish. You won't regret it!

Makes: 1 quart
Prep time: 10 minutes
Cook time: 15 minutes

1 POUND TOMATILLOS, HALVED AND PEELED

3 GARLIC CLOVES, FINELY CHOPPED

2 JALAPEÑO PEPPERS

1 SERRANO PEPPER

1 MEDIUM WHITE ONION, HALVED

¾ CUP ROUGHLY CHOPPED FRESH CILANTRO

3 TABLESPOONS FRESHLY SQUEEZED LIME JUICE

SALT

1   Preheat the oven to 425°F.

2   Line a baking sheet with parchment paper. Arrange the tomatillos, garlic, and peppers on the prepared sheet.

3   Place the sheet in the oven on the center rack and roast for 12 to 15 minutes or until charred.

4   Remove from the oven and let cool.

5   Transfer the ingredients from the baking sheet to a high-speed blender and add the onion, cilantro, and lime juice. Pulse until the sauce reaches the desired consistency.

6   Add salt to taste.

7   Store in a sealed container in the refrigerator for up to 3 weeks.

Storage Tip: The sauce is great served immediately alongside tortilla chips, but the flavors will continue to meld in the refrigerator. The more time you let it sit, the tastier it becomes.

ANCHO HOT SAUCE

This delicious sauce is always a crowd favorite on Taco Tuesdays. I have also found it to be a joy to put on pizza and hamburgers. Try it out on some of your favorite foods and see for yourself!

Makes: about 1 quart
Prep time: 15 minutes
Cook time: 15 minutes

1½ CUPS CHOPPED CARROTS

2 CUPS CHOPPED RED JALAPEÑO PEPPERS OR RED FRESNO PEPPERS

6 WHOLE CLOVES GARLIC

½ CUP APPLE CIDER VINEGAR

½ TEASPOON DRIED OREGANO

2 TABLESPOONS KOSHER SALT, PLUS MORE TO TASTE

½ TEASPOON GROUND CUMIN

2 TABLESPOONS ANCHO CHILI POWDER

SALT

1 In a large saucepan, combine the carrots, peppers, garlic, vinegar, oregano, salt, cumin, and chili powder, and bring to a boil over medium heat.

2 Reduce the heat and simmer for 10 minutes, stirring constantly.

3 Transfer the contents of the saucepan into a high-speed blender and puree.

4 Add salt to taste. Blend again, as necessary.

5 Transfer the hot sauce to a glass bottle.

6 Store in the refrigerator for up to 1 week.

Ingredient Tip: For a thicker sauce, use less vinegar. For a thinner sauce, add water until you reach your desired thickness.

CREAMY JALAPEÑO SAUCE

This is one of my favorite hot sauce recipes, and I love that it requires only four ingredients. I find it to be a perfect addition to tacos, pizza, burgers, hot dogs, and just about anything else you can think of. The versatility of this sauce is what makes it so popular.

12 GREEN JALAPEÑO PEPPERS
2 GARLIC CLOVES
½ CUP VEGETABLE OIL
2 TABLESPOONS KOSHER SALT

Makes: about 1 quart
Prep time: 10 minutes
Cook time: 10 minutes

1   Fill a large saucepan half full of water; then add the jalapeños and bring to a boil over medium heat. Cook until soft.

2   Remove the pan from the heat, cool, and drain, reserving the water. (You may need it for thinning the sauce.)

3   Add the jalapeños, garlic, oil, and salt to a high-speed blender. Puree until smooth and creamy.

4   Fill a squeeze bottle and enjoy! Store in the refrigerator for up to 3 weeks.

Serving Tip: For a thinner sauce, add some of the reserved water, little by little, and reblend the sauce until you've reached the desired thickness.

Ingredient Tip: Substitute serrano peppers for a spicier sauce.

HAWAIIAN CHILE PEPPER WATER

It is customary to find chile pepper water on most tables in the Hawaiian Islands. Although there are several ways to make this sauce, it is super-easy to make a delicious and authentic version using only five ingredients.

Makes: 1 pint
Prep time: 5 minutes

2 CUPS WATER

2 TABLESPOONS WHITE VINEGAR

4 TO 5 HAWAIIAN CHILE PEPPERS

1 CLOVE FRESH GARLIC

SALT

1   Put the water, vinegar, peppers, garlic, and salt in a high-speed blender and liquefy.

2   Add more salt if needed and blend again.

3   Transfer the sauce to a sterilized bottle.

4   Store in a refrigerator for up to 1 month.

Storage Tip: This sauce can be cooked to increase its shelf life. Simply follow the hot-fill bottling procedures on page 36.

NEW MEXICO GREEN CHILE HOT SAUCE

I enjoy using this sauce at breakfast, specifically on eggs and potatoes, but it can be used with any meal. Try it on enchiladas, roasted potatoes, meats, or tacos.

Makes: 3 cups
Prep time: 5 minutes
Cook time: 10 minutes

2 TABLESPOONS VEGETABLE OR CANOLA OIL

3 GARLIC CLOVES, MINCED

$\frac{1}{2}$ WHITE ONION, CHOPPED

$1\frac{1}{2}$ TABLESPOON FLOUR

$\frac{1}{4}$ TEASPOON GROUND CUMIN

$1\frac{1}{2}$ CUPS CHICKEN STOCK

1 CUP CHOPPED NEW MEXICO PEPPERS (ROASTED FRESH OR CANNED)

$\frac{1}{4}$ TEASPOON DRIED OREGANO (OPTIONAL)

KOSHER SALT

FRESHLY GROUND BLACK PEPPER

1. In a medium saucepan, heat the oil and add the garlic and onion. Sauté over medium heat until the onion is soft and fragrant.

2. Stir in the flour, cumin, and chicken stock and simmer over medium heat until the liquid is smooth.

3. Add the roasted or canned peppers and oregano, if desired, and simmer for 5 minutes.

4. Add salt and pepper to taste.

5. Cool and serve.

6. Store in a sealed container in the refrigerator for up to 3 days.

Serving Tip: This sauce can be reheated and is always best served warm.

GARLIC HABANERO SAUCE

I love anything with garlic in it. I especially love when the garlic is overpronounced in a sauce. I think you'll find that this sauce is a good accompaniment to just about any meal, but personally I happen to enjoy it on pasta!

Makes: 1 quart
Prep time: 5 minutes
Cook time: 45 minutes

5 HABANERO PEPPERS, SLICED
20 TO 25 FRESH GARLIC CLOVES
1 TABLESPOON VEGETABLE OIL
1 MEDIUM WHITE ONION, CHOPPED
4 CUPS WHITE VINEGAR
1 CUP WATER
2 TABLESPOONS WHITE SUGAR
½ CUP FRESHLY SQUEEZED LIME JUICE
1 TABLESPOON GARLIC POWDER
SALT

1 Preheat the oven to 425°F.

2 Line a baking sheet with parchment paper. On the prepared sheet, arrange the habaneros and garlic cloves and sprinkle with the oil.

3 Place in the oven and roast for 15 minutes or until slightly charred. Set aside.

4 In a nonreactive medium saucepan, combine the roasted peppers and garlic, onion, vinegar, water, sugar, lime juice, and garlic powder. Bring to a simmer over medium heat and cook for 20 minutes, stirring occasionally.

5 Transfer the sauce to the bowl of a food processor and puree until smooth.

6 Add salt to taste. Blend again, if necessary.

7 Bottle in sterilized jars.

8 Store in the refrigerator for up to 1 month.

Substitution Tip: Substitute yellow fatalii peppers for a spicier sauce.

GARLIC REAPER HOT SAUCE

As the name implies, this hot sauce is not for the faint of heart. As a matter of fact, you'd better be a well-seasoned pro at hot sauce eating before trying this recipe out. Beware! Don't say I didn't warn you!

Makes: about 1 quart
Prep time: 15 minutes
Cook time: 35 minutes

15 FRESH CAROLINA REAPER PEPPERS

10 TO 12 FRESH GARLIC CLOVES, DICED

1 LARGE WHITE ONION, CHOPPED

2 TEASPOONS KOSHER SALT, PLUS MORE TO TASTE

½ CUP WHITE VINEGAR

½ CUP APPLE CIDER VINEGAR

1 CUP WATER

SALT

1   In a nonreactive medium saucepan, combine the peppers, garlic, onion, salt, vinegars, and water.

2   Bring to a boil over medium heat; then reduce the heat and simmer for 30 minutes. Set aside to cool.

3   Place the cooled ingredients into a high-speed blender and puree until they reach the desired consistency.

4   Add salt to taste. Blend again, if necessary.

5   Transfer to sterilized bottles and store in the refrigerator for up to 3 weeks.

Preparation Tip: Make sure to wear gloves when handling super-hot peppers like the Carolina Reaper.

CHAPTER FIVE:

South America and Central America

South and Central Americans predominantly use a pepper called an aji pepper that is said to have been around for thousands of years. In Colombia, a red sauce called aji picante is used to spice up beans, meats, plantains, and empanadas. It's made with the aji pepper, tomatoes, cilantro, and onion. In Venezuela, however, a green avocado-type of salsa is used for virtually the same dishes. It is made with bell pepper, avocado, cilantro, and parsley and is much more mild than the aji picante. Here are some recipes from these regions for you to try.

ARGENTINEAN SPICY CHIMICHURRI

This is a beautiful sauce that takes about 10 minutes to make. This spicy recipe is sure to please all palates and complements many foods. It's particularly good on steak.

Makes: about 1 pint
Prep time: 10 minutes

1 CUP ROUGHLY CHOPPED AND PACKED FRESH PARSLEY LEAVES

2 TABLESPOONS ROUGHLY CHOPPED FRESH OREGANO LEAVES

5 GARLIC CLOVES, MINCED

½ CUP EXTRA-VIRGIN OLIVE OIL

2 TABLESPOONS WHITE WINE VINEGAR

1 TEASPOON RED PEPPER FLAKES

½ TABLESPOON KOSHER SALT, PLUS MORE TO TASTE

½ TABLESPOON FRESHLY GROUND BLACK PEPPER, PLUS MORE TO TASTE

1 In the bowl of a small food processor, put the parsley, oregano, and garlic and pulse to mix.

2 Pour the mixture into a small bowl and add in the olive oil, vinegar, red pepper flakes, salt, and pepper. Mix to combine.

3 Add additional salt and pepper to taste.

4 Serve immediately or store in a refrigerator for up to 2 days.

Substitution Tip: You can use 2 teaspoons of dried oregano leaves in place of the fresh oregano.
Serving Tip: If chilled, return to room temperature before serving.

SPICY FERMENTED COLOMBIAN HOT SAUCE

This vibrant sauce is sure to fire up those taste buds. While it takes a bit of patience to make, since you need to let it rest for 24 hours, I promise that it's sure worth the wait!

Makes: 1 pint
Prep time: 15 minutes, plus 24 hours of rest time

2 JALAPEÑO PEPPERS, MINCED

½ CUP FINELY MINCED FRESH CILANTRO

¼ CUP FINELY MINCED SCALLIONS

½ TEASPOON SALT

½ TEASPOON WHITE SUGAR

¼ CUP WATER

½ CUP WHITE VINEGAR

2 TABLESPOONS FRESHLY SQUEEZED LIME JUICE

1   Combine the peppers, cilantro, and scallions in a sealable jar.

2   Pour in the salt and sugar.

3   In a small mixing bowl, combine water, vinegar, and lime juice and then pour mixture into the jar to cover the other ingredients.

4   Seal the jar and let it sit in a dark, cool place for 24 hours.

5   Serve or refrigerate for up to 1 month.

Ingredient Tip: Use a serrano or habanero for added heat.

BOLIVIAN HOT SAUCE

This Bolivian hot sauce is used on just about every dish: soups, beef, chicken, and fish to name a few. It's easy and takes no time to make.

Makes: 2 cups
Prep time: 10 minutes

5 TOMATOES, QUARTERED AND SEEDED

2 SERRANO CHILE PEPPERS

4 FRESH BASIL LEAVES

2 SPRIGS FRESH CILANTRO

1 TABLESPOONS SALT, PLUS MORE TO TASTE

3 TABLESPOONS EXTRA-VIRGIN OLIVE OIL

1   Combine all the ingredients in a high-speed blender.

2   Puree until smooth and add more salt to taste. Refrigerate for up to 1 week.

EL SALVADORIAN SALSA ROJA

I think that you will find this to be an amazing sauce that brings flavor and roasted notes to any food that it graces. Use it on empanadas or serve it with tortilla chips.

Makes: 2 cups
Prep time: 10 minutes
Cook time: 10 minutes

4 TABLESPOONS VEGETABLE OIL

¼ CUP CHOPPED YELLOW ONION

2 GARLIC CLOVES, MINCED

2 JALAPEÑO PEPPERS, CHOPPED

2½ CUPS TOMATOES, SEEDED AND CHOPPED

1 TABLESPOON DRIED OREGANO

½ CUP FRESH CILANTRO

SALT

FRESHLY GROUND BLACK PEPPER

1   In a medium saucepan, heat the oil over medium-high heat. Add the onion, garlic, and jalapeño and sauté for 3 minutes.

2   Stir in tomatoes and oregano. Simmer for 5 minutes and let cool.

3   Transfer the sauce to a high-speed blender and add the cilantro. Puree until smooth.

4   Add salt and pepper to taste. Refrigerate for up to 1 week.

Ingredient Tip: Substitute serrano peppers for a spicier version.

AJI AMARILLO HOT SAUCE

An easy recipe that my neighbor taught me. We use this sauce on eggs, enchiladas, and sometimes even hot dogs.

Makes: 2 cups
Prep time: 15 minutes, plus 4 to 6 hours of rest time

1 AJI AMARILLO PEPPER (I USE YELLOW FATALII PEPPERS)

½ CUP MAYONNAISE

¼ CUP SOUR CREAM

2 TABLESPOONS KETCHUP

3 SCALLIONS, WHITES ONLY, FINELY CHOPPED

JUICE OF 1 LIME

SALT

FRESHLY GROUND BLACK PEPPER

1 Combine the aji amarillo, mayonnaise, sour cream, ketchup, scallions, and lime juice in a high-speed blender and pulse until smooth.

2 Add salt and pepper to taste.

3 Let sit 4 to 6 hours to allow flavors to combine.

4 Serve immediately, or refrigerate for 1 to 2 weeks.

AVOCADO, CILANTRO, AND LIME HOT SAUCE

I am a huge fan of Central American crema-style sauces. These condiments are great for fish tacos, fresh ceviche, and even green salads. I hope you enjoy this one as much as I do!

Makes: 1 quart
Prep time: 5 minutes

2 MEDIUM TO LARGE RIPE AVOCADOS, PITTED, PEELED, AND SLICED

16 OUNCES MEXICAN OR HONDURAN CREMA

2 CUPS FRESH CILANTRO

1 CUP FRESHLY SQUEEZED LIME JUICE

1 JALAPEÑO PEPPER, SEEDED AND MEMBRANES REMOVED

2 TABLESPOONS VEGETABLE OIL

SALT

1   Combine the avocados, crema, cilantro, lime juice, jalapeño, and oil in a high-speed blender and puree until smooth.

2   Add salt to taste. Blend again, if necessary.

3   Transfer the sauce to a plastic squeeze bottle.

4   Store in the refrigerator for only up to 1 day due to the speed at which the avocado will spoil.

Substitution Tip: Substitute garlic salt for a different spin on this recipe, or try substituting your favorite green pepper for jalapeños.

COLOMBIAN AJI HOT SAUCE

This sauce is a staple in all Colombian households. Colombians use it as much as Americans use ketchup. Try it with empanadas, arepas, or tacos. You won't be disappointed!

Makes: 1 quart
Prep time:
20 minutes, plus
30 to 45 minutes of
rest time

2 BUNCHES GREEN ONIONS, HALF OF THE WHITE PARTS AND ALL THE GREEN PARTS FINELY CHOPPED

1 LARGE TOMATO, DICED

¼ BUNCH FINELY CHOPPED FRESH CILANTRO

4 JALAPEÑO PEPPERS

2 GARLIC CLOVES, DICED

¼ CUP WHITE VINEGAR

½ CUP WATER

1 TABLESPOON VEGETABLE OIL

SALT

1 In a large mixing bowl, combine the onions, tomato, cilantro, jalapeños, and garlic.

2 Add vinegar, water, oil, and salt to taste.

3 Cover and place in the refrigerator for about 30 to 45 minutes to allow flavors to combine.

4 Add more salt, if needed. Stir and serve.

5 Store in a sealed container in the refrigerator for up to 1 week.

Ingredient Tip: Add more water if it tastes too vinegary, or add more vinegar if it tastes too watery.

PERUVIAN AJI VERDE

After you've given this one a go, I think that you will agree that this Peruvian hot sauce is out-of-this-world good! Its creamy consistency is an amazing addition when drizzled on tacos and used to flavor meats. This is another one of my favorite sauces to make.

Makes: 2 cups
Prep time: 15 minutes

2 JALAPEÑO PEPPERS, SEEDED AND MEMBRANES REMOVED

2 CUPS FRESH CILANTRO

¾ CUP MAYONNAISE

3 GARLIC CLOVES

2 TABLESPOONS FRESHLY SQUEEZED LIME JUICE

⅓ CUP COTIJA OR PARMESAN CHEESE, GRATED

SALT

1   In a high-speed blender, combine the jalapeños, cilantro, mayonnaise, garlic, lime juice, and cheese and puree until smooth.

2   Taste and add salt, if needed. Blend again, if necessary.

3   Store in a sealed container in the refrigerator for up to 2 weeks.

Ingredient Tip: Try adding a splash of vegetable oil to the blender if the mixture is too bold.

SPICY CHILEAN PEBRE

This condiment from Chile is in the South American tradition. It's great on just about every-thing Chilean, especially sea bass.

Makes: 1 pint
Prep time: 10 minutes

4 SERRANO PEPPERS, CHOPPED

½ MEDIUM WHITE ONION, CHOPPED

5 GARLIC CLOVES, MINCED

¼ CUP CHOPPED FRESH CILANTRO

2 TABLESPOONS WHITE WINE VINEGAR

½ CUP EXTRA-VIRGIN OLIVE OIL, DIVIDED

SALT

FRESHLY GROUND BLACK PEPPER

1   In a high-speed blender, combine the serrano peppers, onion, garlic, cilantro, vinegar, ¼ cup olive oil, and salt and pepper to taste. Puree until smooth.

2   Slowly add the remaining olive oil until the sauce reaches the desired consistency.

3   Refrigerate for up to 1 week and allow flavors to blend.

Ingredient Tip: Use seeded jalapeño peppers for a milder sauce.

BELIZEAN HABANERO HOT SAUCE

If you've ever tried the Marie Sharp's brand of hot sauces, then you've tried Belizean sauces. People ask for it by name, and it's sometimes hard to get. Why not make your own?

Makes: 1 quart
Prep time: 15 minutes
Cook time:
20 minutes

3 GARLIC CLOVES, CHOPPED

1 MEDIUM WHITE ONION, CHOPPED

1½ CUPS CHOPPED CARROTS

2 CUPS WATER

10 ORANGE HABANERO PEPPERS, MINCED

3 TABLESPOONS FRESHLY SQUEEZED LIME JUICE

3 TABLESPOONS WHITE VINEGAR

2 TABLESPOONS SALT

1 In a large saucepan, sauté the garlic and onion until aromatic.

2 Add the carrots and water and bring to a boil. Reduce to a simmer and cook 15 minutes or until the carrots are soft.

3 Remove from the heat and let cool.

4 Add the habanero peppers, lime juice, vinegar, and salt.

5 Transfer everything to a high-speed blender and puree until smooth.

6 Pour into sterilized bottles and enjoy! This will keep in the refrigerator for up to 3 weeks.

Ingredient Tip: Add exotic fruits like mango or papaya when blending.

ECUADORIAN HOT SAUCE

This Ecuadorian staple, otherwise known as aji criollo, uses aji peppers native to Ecuador. If aji peppers are unavailable, I like to use red habanero peppers instead.

Makes: 2 cups
Prep time: 15 minutes

4 AJI PEPPERS OR RED HABANEROS, CHOPPED

½ CUP FRESH CHOPPED CILANTRO

¾ CUP WATER

4 GARLIC CLOVES

¼ CUP FRESHLY SQUEEZED LIME JUICE

2 SCALLIONS (WHITE PARTS), CHOPPED

SALT

1   In a high-speed blender, combine the peppers, cilantro, water, garlic, and lime juice and puree until the sauce reaches the desired consistency.

2   Add the scallions and add salt to taste. Pulse briefly.

3   Pour the sauce into a sealable container and store in the refrigerator for up to 1 week.

Ingredient Tip: Use 1 tablespoon white vinegar for a bolder taste.

CHAPTER SIX:

The Caribbean

Caribbean hot sauces are a staple in just about every household. The native Scotch bonnet and Scorpion peppers are used in several sauces and are some of the spiciest peppers in existence. As such, you'll notice that all of these sauces are *hot*! Mixed with tropical fruit such as mango, papaya, or pineapple, these sauces are great additions to soups, fish, and stews and are even used as marinades.

CARIBBEAN HOT PEPPER SAUCE

This is a very easy recipe to make. It only requires four ingredients and is used as a base for many Caribbean-style sauces.

1 POUND SCOTCH BONNET PEPPERS
1½ TABLESPOONS KOSHER SALT
2 CUPS WHITE VINEGAR
2 TABLESPOONS VEGETABLE OIL

Makes: 2½ cups
Prep time: 10 minutes
Cook time: 15 minutes,
plus 24 hours of
rest time

1 In a high-speed blender, combine the peppers, salt, and vinegar and puree until smooth.

2 In a medium pot, heat the oil over medium-high heat.

3 Add the blender mixture to the pot and bring to a boil, stirring constantly.

4 Transfer the sauce to sterilized glass bottles and let them sit in the refrigerator for 24 hours to allow the flavors to blend. Store in the refrigerator for up to 3 months.

Recipe Tip: Wear a mask and goggles when cooking this sauce, turn on all the fans, and open the windows.

CARIBBEAN JERK MANGO HOT SAUCE

This is great as a dipping sauce for chicken and shrimp, or used as a marinade! This hot sauce is a spicy island favorite that has a true front-of-the-tongue burn that lasts for a while!

Makes: 1 quart
Prep time: 10 minutes
Cook time: 15 minutes

3 TABLESPOONS VEGETABLE OIL

2 GARLIC CLOVES, MINCED

1 SMALL RED ONION, CHOPPED

8 HABANERO PEPPERS, CHOPPED

2 RIPE MANGOS, PEELED, PITTED, AND CHOPPED

1 CUP APPLE CIDER VINEGAR

2 TABLESPOONS BROWN SUGAR

1½ TABLESPOONS JERK SEASONING

½ CUP WATER

1 In a large saucepan, heat the oil over medium-high heat.

2 Sauté the garlic, red onion, and habanero peppers until the onion is translucent, 2 to 3 minutes.

3 Add the mangos, vinegar, brown sugar, jerk seasoning, and water. Bring to a simmer, and cook for an additional 10 minutes.

4 Transfer the sauce to a high-speed blender and process until smooth. Pour into a sealable container and keep in the refrigerator for up to 3 weeks.

Recipe Tip: The longer this sauce sits in the refrigerator, the deeper the flavors will become.

Substitution Tip: Substitute chopped pineapple for the mangos.

GINGER-MANGO HOT SAUCE

The pickled ginger makes this an interesting take on a hot sauce. I take this sauce to my local sushi restaurant and use it on sushi and sashimi!

Makes: 1 pint
Prep time: 10 minutes
Cook time:
20 minutes

2 HABANERO PEPPERS, CHOPPED

1 MANGO, PEELED, SEEDED, AND CHOPPED

2 TABLESPOONS PICKLED GINGER SLICES, FROM A JAR

1 CUP APPLE CIDER VINEGAR

1/3 CUP WATER

1 TEASPOON KOSHER SALT

1 TABLESPOON WHITE SUGAR

1   In a food processor or high-speed blender, combine the peppers, mango, pickled ginger, vinegar, water, salt, and sugar and puree until smooth.

2   Transfer the sauce into a medium saucepan and bring to a boil over medium heat. Reduce the heat and simmer for 15 minutes. Remove from the heat and allow to cool.

3   Pour the sauce into a sealable container or bottle and store in the refrigerator for up to 3 weeks.

Substitution Tip: Substitute 1 teaspoon ground ginger for the pickled ginger.
Ingredient Tip: Add more habaneros for a spicier sauce.

JAMAICAN-STYLE HOT SAUCE

This one will make you think of a cool breeze on the isle of Jamaica. We use this hot sauce on jerk chicken, grilled lamb, and steaks. I especially like to marinate my grilled chicken in it a few hours before cooking!

Makes: 3 cups
Prep time: 5 minutes

3 HABANERO PEPPERS, CHOPPED

1 SMALL SWEET ONION, CHOPPED

1 CARROT, CHOPPED

½ CUP FROZEN MANGO CHUNKS

½ CUP FROZEN PINEAPPLE CHUNKS

4 GARLIC CLOVES

½ TEASPOON GROUND CUMIN

1 CUP FRESHLY SQUEEZED LIME JUICE

¼ CUP APPLE CIDER VINEGAR

1 TABLESPOON KOSHER SALT, PLUS MORE TO TASTE

1   In a food processor or high-speed blender, combine the peppers, onion, carrot, mango, pineapple, garlic, cumin, lime juice, vinegar, and salt and puree until smooth.

2   Add additional salt to taste. Pulse briefly, if necessary.

3   Pour the sauce into a sealable container or bottle and store in the refrigerator for up to 2 weeks.

Substitution Tip: Substitute Scotch bonnets for the habanero peppers.

Serving Tip: Strain if you want a thinner sauce.

MANGO-HABANERO HOT SAUCE

This is a home run hot sauce for just about anything! This sauce is especially good on coconut shrimp, chicken, and fish dishes.

Makes: about 1 quart
Prep time: 15 minutes
Cook time:
20 minutes

4 HABANERO PEPPERS

6 GARLIC CLOVES

1 SMALL YELLOW ONION, CHOPPED

1 RIPE MANGO, PITTED, PEELED, AND CHOPPED

½ CUP APPLE CIDER VINEGAR

½ CUP WATER

1 TEASPOON KOSHER SALT

1 TEASPOON GROUND GINGER

½ TEASPOON GROUND ALLSPICE

¼ TEASPOON GROUND CUMIN

3 TABLESPOONS HONEY

1 In a food processor or high-speed blender, combine the peppers, garlic, onion, mango, vinegar, water, salt, ginger, allspice, cumin, and honey and puree until smooth.

2 Transfer the sauce to a medium saucepan and bring to a boil over medium heat. Reduce the heat and simmer for 15 minutes. Remove from the heat and allow to cool.

3 Pour the sauce into a sealable container or bottle and store in the refrigerator for up to 3 weeks.

Substitution Tip: Substitute Scotch bonnets for the habanero peppers.

PAPAYA HOT SAUCE

This sauce reminds me of my childhood, growing up in Hawaii, eating papayas as snacks—but mixed with my passion: hot sauce! It's perfect for use on fish and curry.

Makes: 1 pint
Prep time: 15 minutes
Cook time: 5 minutes

1 RIPE PAPAYA, PEELED, DESEEDED, AND CHOPPED

1 SMALL WHITE ONION, CHOPPED

3 GARLIC CLOVES

1 TABLESPOON GROUND GINGER

5 SCOTCH BONNET PEPPERS, CHOPPED

1 TABLESPOON MUSTARD POWDER

½ TEASPOON GROUND TURMERIC

1 TABLESPOON HONEY

¼ CUP WATER

¾ CUP APPLE CIDER VINEGAR

1 TABLESPOON KOSHER SALT

1 In a food processor or high-speed blender, combine the papaya, onion, garlic, ginger, peppers, mustard powder, turmeric, honey, and water and puree.

2 Transfer the papaya mixture to a medium mixing bowl and set aside.

3 In a small saucepan, combine the vinegar and salt and bring to a boil over medium heat. Remove from the heat and allow to cool slightly.

4 Pour the vinegar-and-salt mixture over the papaya mixture and stir until well combined.

5 Pour the sauce into a sealed container or bottle and store in the refrigerator for up to 4 weeks.

Substitution Tip: Substitute mango or peaches for the papaya.

PINEAPPLE-HABANERO SAUCE

This sauce is perfect for spicing up your margaritas or adding some additional flavor to your Baja-style fish tacos!

Makes: 1 pint
Prep time: 10 minutes
Cook time: 15 minutes

4 HABANERO PEPPERS
1 (14.5-OUNCE) CAN PINEAPPLE CHUNKS
½ CUP FRESHLY SQUEEZED LIME JUICE
1 CUP VINEGAR
1 TABLESPOON KOSHER SALT
1 CUP FRESH CILANTRO

1   In a food processor or high-speed blender, combine the peppers, pineapple, lime juice, vinegar, salt, and cilantro and puree until smooth.

2   Transfer the sauce to a medium saucepan and bring to a boil over medium heat. Reduce the heat and simmer for 10 minutes. Remove from the heat and allow to cool.

3   Pour the sauce into bottles or into a sealable container and store in the refrigerator for up to 3 weeks.

Ingredient Tip: Try adding roasted pineapple for a different flavor profile.

PUERTO RICAN PIQUE SAUCE

If you like it spicy, then this is the recipe for you! This recipe is a surefire winner when making dishes like tostones (battered and deep-fried sliced plantains) and arroz con pollo.

Makes: about
2 quarts
Prep time: 20 minutes
Cook time: 5 minutes

2 TABLESPOONS EXTRA-VIRGIN OLIVE OIL

1 WHITE ONION, FINELY CHOPPED, DIVIDED

15 HABANERO PEPPERS, ROUGHLY CHOPPED

10 FRESH GARLIC CLOVES, MINCED

1 CUP PINEAPPLE JUICE

JUICE OF 1 LIME

¼ CUP WHITE TEQUILA

¼ CUP WHITE VINEGAR

10 SPRIGS ROUGHLY CHOPPED FRESH CILANTRO

1 TEASPOON WHITE SUGAR

1 TEASPOON DRIED OREGANO

1 TEASPOON SALT

1 TEASPOON FRESHLY GROUND BLACK PEPPER

1 TEASPOON CACAO POWDER

½ TEASPOON GROUND CUMIN

1   In a large saucepan, heat the olive oil over medium-high heat and add half of the onion with the habanero peppers and garlic. Sauté until tender.

2   Transfer the onion mixture to a high-speed blender and add all of the remaining ingredients.

continued

3 Blend until smooth.

4 Immediately transfer the sauce to sterilized bottles and let them let stand for 1 week. This will allow the flavors to meld together and will bring out a more well-rounded taste. The sauce will keep for 4 weeks in the refrigerator.

Ingredient Tip: Substitute scorpion or Carolina reaper peppers for the habaneros for a much spicier dish.

ROASTED PINEAPPLE AND HOT PEPPER SAUCE

A favorite sauce of mine that I like to use on fish tacos or as a marinade for chicken and pork! Your family will love you for this one!

Makes: 3 cups
Prep time: 20 minutes
Cook time: 15 minutes

2 CUPS ROASTED PINEAPPLE (ROAST FRESH OR CANNED SLICES ON A GRILL)

1 JALAPEÑO PEPPER, CHOPPED

1 SERRANO PEPPER, CHOPPED

1 HABANERO PEPPER, CHOPPED

2 ROMA TOMATOES, CHOPPED

1 SMALL RED ONION, CHOPPED

6 GARLIC CLOVES

⅓ CUP CHOPPED FRESH CILANTRO

¼ CUP FRESHLY SQUEEZED LIME JUICE

½ CUP WHITE WINE VINEGAR

1 TABLESPOON KOSHER SALT

1 TABLESPOON FRESHLY GROUND BLACK PEPPER

1 In a food processor, combine the pineapple, peppers, tomatoes, onion, garlic, cilantro, lime juice, vinegar, salt, and pepper and puree until smooth.

2 Transfer to a medium saucepan and bring to a boil over medium heat. Reduce the heat and simmer for 10 minutes. Remove from the heat.

3 Bottle the sauce in sterilized containers when the sauce is at least 180°F and store in the refrigerator for up to 3 weeks.

Ingredient Tip: For a thinner sauce, add water or vinegar.

SCOTCH BONNET HOT SAUCE WITH PEACHES AND MANGO

My family likes to use this one on shrimp ceviche, but it's also outstanding on fish, chicken, and pork!

Makes: about 1 quart
Prep time: 10 minutes
Cook time:
20 minutes

8 SCOTCH BONNET PEPPERS, CHOPPED

1 POUND ROMA TOMATOES, CHOPPED

4 GARLIC CLOVES

1 FRESH MANGO, PITTED, PEELED, AND CHOPPED

1 PEACH, PITTED, PEELED, AND CHOPPED

1 TABLESPOON MUSTARD POWDER

1 TABLESPOON KOSHER SALT

3 TABLESPOONS HONEY

¼ TEASPOON GROUND CINNAMON

¼ TEASPOON GROUND NUTMEG

½ CUP APPLE CIDER VINEGAR

1 In a food processor, combine the peppers, tomatoes, garlic, mango, peach, mustard powder, salt, honey, cinnamon, nutmeg, and vinegar and puree until smooth.

2 Transfer the sauce to a medium saucepan and bring to a boil over medium heat. Reduce the heat and simmer for 15 minutes. Remove from the heat.

3 Bottle the sauce in sterilized containers when the sauce is at least 180°F and store in the refrigerator for up to 3 months.

Substitution Tip: Substitute habanero peppers for Scotch bonnet peppers.

SPICY CURRY HOT SAUCE

This is a hot sauce that's a regional favorite for spicing up curry or any other soup or stew. I particularly love the lemongrass flavor!

Makes: 1 cup
Prep time: 15 minutes
Cook time: 15 minutes

20 SCOTCH BONNET PEPPERS

5 OUNCES RED BELL PEPPER

5 OUNCES GREEN BELL PEPPER

8 GARLIC CLOVES

2 STALKS FRESH LEMONGRASS (BULBS ONLY)

$\frac{1}{2}$ CUP APPLE CIDER VINEGAR

$\frac{3}{4}$ CUP WATER

2 TABLESPOONS FRESHLY GROUND BLACK PEPPER

1 TABLESPOON KOSHER SALT

1$\frac{1}{2}$ TABLESPOONS CURRY POWDER

1   In a food processor, combine the peppers, garlic, lemongrass, vinegar, water, black pepper, salt, and curry powder and puree until smooth.

2   Transfer the sauce to a medium saucepan and bring to a boil over medium heat. Reduce the heat and simmer for 10 minutes. Remove from the heat and allow to cool.

3   Pour the sauce into a sealed container or bottle and store in the refrigerator for up to 3 weeks.

Substitution Tip: Substitute habanero peppers for the Scotch bonnets. Also consider using lemongrass paste or powder if fresh lemongrass is unavailable.

Ingredient Tip: For a thinner sauce, add more water.

CHAPTER SEVEN:

Asia

Many people associate Asian-style hot sauces with sriracha, which is also known as "rooster sauce" (see page 11). Hot chile oil is another staple in many Asian homes. Hot chile oil historically requires only two ingredients—soybean oil and red chili flakes—but you can get creative and add garlic or soy sauce. In this chapter I'm going to share some other cool and popular Asian-inspired hot sauce recipes. I'm getting hungry just thinking about it!

SWEET AND SPICY ASIAN-STYLE HOT SAUCE

This recipe is another Asian classic that will complement any dish! Sweet and spicy is my favorite go-to for hot sauces. Try using it on fried rice, stir-fries, and eggs.

Makes: 1 cup
Prep time: 5 minutes
Cook time: 15 minutes

4 TABLESPOONS SRIRACHA

4 TABLESPOONS HONEY

4 TABLESPOONS SOY SAUCE

2 TABLESPOONS RICE WINE VINEGAR

½ CUP FRESHLY SQUEEZED LIME JUICE

3 GARLIC CLOVES, MINCED

6 TABLESPOONS HOISIN SAUCE

1   In a medium saucepan, combine the sriracha, honey, soy sauce, vinegar, lime juice, garlic, and hoisin and bring to a simmer over medium heat.

2   Simmer for 10 minutes, stirring occasionally. Remove from heat and allow to cool.

3   Pour the sauce into a bottle or sealable container and refrigerate for up to 3 weeks.

Ingredient Tip: Add a teaspoon of ghost pepper powder for a spicier sauce.

SPICY TERIYAKI SAUCE

Use it as a dipping sauce or a marinade or drizzle it on everything! It's perfect for stir-fries, chicken wings, and pork shanks.

Makes: 1 quart
Prep time: 5 minutes
Cook time: 15 minutes

1 CUP SOY SAUCE

1½ CUPS WATER, DIVIDED

½ CUP BROWN SUGAR

3 TABLESPOONS HONEY

1 TABLESPOON MINCED FRESH GINGER

1 TEASPOON SESAME OIL

2 TABLESPOONS GARLIC, MINCED

5 TABLESPOONS MIRIN

3 TABLESPOONS CRUSHED RED PEPPER FLAKES

1 TABLESPOON CORNSTARCH

1   In a large saucepan, combine the soy sauce, 1 cup of water, sugar, honey, ginger, sesame oil, garlic, mirin, and chili flakes. Mix together and cook over medium heat for 10 minutes, stirring constantly. Remove from the heat and set aside.

2   In a small mixing bowl, make a slurry (a kind of thickener) by whisking the remaining ½ cup of water and the cornstarch together.

3   Add the slurry to the contents of the pan and stir until well combined.

4   Return the pan to the stove over high heat and bring to a boil, stirring constantly. Reduce the heat and simmer until sauce thickens. Remove from the heat and let cool.

5   Transfer the sauce to a bottle or sealable container and store in the refrigerator for up to 2 weeks.

Ingredient Tip: Add more chili flakes if you want it spicier.

SPICY THAI PEANUT SAUCE

In as little as 5 minutes you can have a great spicy Thai peanut sauce that is great on egg rolls and noodles. I personally like to use this sauce when I stir-fry vegetables and meats.

Makes: ¾ pint
Prep time: 5 Minutes

½ CUP CREAMY PEANUT BUTTER

1 TABLESPOON RICE WINE VINEGAR

1 TABLESPOON SESAME OIL

2 TABLESPOONS SOY SAUCE

2 TABLESPOONS SAMBAL OELEK (STORE-BOUGHT OR HOMEMADE, SEE PAGE 94)

1 TABLESPOON HONEY

1 TEASPOON GROUND GINGER

1 TEASPOON GROUND CAYENNE

1 TEASPOON GARLIC POWDER

1   In a large mixing bowl, combine the peanut butter, vinegar, sesame oil, soy sauce, sambal oelek, honey, ginger, cayenne, and garlic powder and whisk together until well combined.

2   Add water to thin out the consistency, if desired.

3   Pour the sauce into a sealable container or bottle and store in the refrigerator for up to 2 weeks.

Ingredient Tip: Add a squeeze of lime juice for extra zest.

SWEET AND SPICY SRIRACHA DIPPING SAUCE

This sauce is great for dipping your egg rolls, spring rolls, and summer rolls! I especially like to use this sauce for pot stickers and fried wontons.

Makes: 1 cup
Prep time: 5 minutes
Cook time: 10 minutes

3 TABLESPOONS SOY SAUCE

4 TABLESPOONS RICE WINE VINEGAR

1 TABLESPOON SRIRACHA SAUCE

2 TEASPOONS SESAME OIL

3 TABLESPOONS WHITE SUGAR

1 In a small bowl, combine the soy sauce, vinegar, sriracha, sesame oil, and white sugar and whisk until well combined.

2 Put in a small saucepan and cook over medium heat for 5 minutes. Remove from the heat and allow to cool.

3 Pour the sauce into a sealable container or bottle and store in the refrigerator for up to 2 weeks.

Ingredient Tip: Add more sriracha sauce to make it spicier.

ASIAN-STYLE CHILE OIL

This is a quick and easy chile oil that you can use in your dishes. Add some to fire up some soups and stews or use on fried rice and noodles!

1 CUP CANOLA OR VEGETABLE OIL

3 OR 4 TABLESPOONS CRUSHED RED PEPPER FLAKES

1 TEASPOON KOSHER SALT

1 TABLESPOON MINCED GARLIC

DASH OF GARLIC POWDER

Makes: 1 cup

Prep time: 5 Minutes

Cook time: 10 Minutes

1   In a small saucepan, combine the vegetable oil, chili flakes, salt, minced garlic, and garlic powder and bring to a simmer over low heat, stirring constantly. Let simmer for about 5 minutes. Remove from the heat and cool.

2   Pour the sauce into a sealable jar and store in the refrigerator for up to 1 month.

Ingredient Tip: Add more chili flakes if you want it spicier.

HOMEMADE SRIRACHA SAUCE

Who doesn't love sriracha sauce when eating any type of Asian food? You see it on just about every table in every restaurant—Asian restaurants or otherwise. Well, now you can make your own! It's super-easy and less salty than the original version.

Makes: 2 quarts
Prep time: 10 minutes
Cook time:
20 minutes

1 POUND (15 TO 20) RED FRESNO PEPPERS, CHOPPED

4 GARLIC CLOVES

2 TEASPOONS KOSHER SALT

2 TEASPOONS BROWN SUGAR

2 TEASPOONS WHITE SUGAR

3 CUPS WHITE VINEGAR

1   In a high-speed blender, combine the peppers, garlic, salt, brown sugar, white sugar, and vinegar and puree until smooth.

2   Transfer the sauce to a large saucepan and bring to a boil over medium-high heat.

3   Turn down the heat and let simmer for 15 minutes, stirring occasionally.

4   Let cool to no more than 180°F and pour into sterilized bottles.

5   Store in the refrigerator for up to 6 months.

Substitution Tip: You can use red jalapeños if you can't find Fresno peppers.

SWEET THAI CHILE SAUCE WITH GARLIC

This sauce is sweet and savory and is a great dipping or stir-fry sauce. This caramelizes well and is good on all meats, including seafood and duck.

Makes: 1 pint
Prep time: 10 minutes
Cook time: 15 minutes

5 RED JALAPEÑO PEPPERS, CHOPPED
4 GARLIC CLOVES
2 TABLESPOONS HONEY
½ CUP WHITE SUGAR, PLUS MORE TO TASTE
1½ CUPS WHITE VINEGAR
1 TABLESPOON KOSHER SALT, PLUS MORE TO TASTE

1 In a food processor, combine the peppers, garlic, honey, sugar, vinegar, and salt and process until smooth.

2 Transfer the sauce to a medium saucepan and bring to a boil over medium heat.

3 Reduce the heat and simmer for 10 minutes, stirring occasionally.

4 Turn off the heat and let cool. Add more sugar and salt as desired.

5 Pour into sterilized bottles or a sealable container and store in the refrigerator for up to 6 weeks.

Ingredient Tip: Use 1 teaspoon xanthan gum (or a cornstarch slurry) to thicken the sauce if desired.
Serving Tip: Consider straining the solids if you want a thinner sauce.

SZECHUAN SAUCE

This 3-minute Szechuan-style sauce not only is easy to make but lasts a week in your refrigerator. Spice it up with more and more crushed red pepper flakes until you reach your favorite spice level! This tastes especially great on chicken wings and fried rice.

Makes: ½ cup
Prep time: 3 minutes

½ CUP SOY SAUCE

2 TABLESPOONS BROWN SUGAR

1 TABLESPOON GARLIC CHILE OIL, STORE-BOUGHT OR HOMEMADE (SEE ASIAN-STYLE CHILE OIL, PAGE 90)

1 TABLESPOON RICE WINE VINEGAR

½ TEASPOON GARLIC POWDER

½ TEASPOON GROUND GINGER

½ TEASPOON CRUSHED RED PEPPER FLAKES

½ TEASPOON CHINESE FIVE-SPICE POWDER

1   In a medium mixing bowl, combine the soy sauce, brown sugar, chile oil, vinegar, garlic powder, ginger, red pepper flakes, and five-spice powder. Whisk well to combine.

2   Pour the sauce into a sealable container and store in a refrigerator for up to 1 week.

Ingredient Tip: Substitute red pepper flakes for 2 ounces of fresh ground scorpion peppers for some serious heat.

SAMBAL OELEK

This chile paste is widely used throughout Asia to spice up all kinds of dishes. Traditionally, it is prepared raw and uncooked, but some prefer to cook it to mellow the flavors.

Makes: 1 pint
Prep time: 5 minutes

¾ POUND RED THAI PEPPERS, CHOPPED
2 TABLESPOONS RICE WINE VINEGAR
1 TABLESPOON KOSHER SALT
1 GARLIC CLOVE

1 In a food processor or high-speed blender, combine the peppers, vinegar, salt, and garlic and puree.

2 Strain out the liquid through a fine-mesh sieve and remove from paste.

3 Transfer the sauce to a jar with an airtight lid and store in a refrigerator for up to 3 weeks.

Substitution Tip: You can substitute red jalapeño, red serrano, or cayenne peppers for the Thai peppers.
Recipe Tip: If you prefer to cook your Sambal Oelek, puree peppers, vinegar, salt, and garlic in a food processor or blender, and add the puree to a small pot, and heat on low for 15 minutes, stirring constantly. Serve immediately and enjoy!

THAI PEPPER HOT SAUCE

This sauce is very similar to sriracha but is a little thinner and, in my opinion, has a more complex flavor. Try it on pizza, burgers, and any Asian-style food.

Makes: 1½ pints
Prep time: 15 minutes
Cook time:
25 minutes

5 GARLIC CLOVES

1 POUND RED THAI PEPPERS

1 CUP WATER

5 TABLESPOONS BROWN SUGAR

1 CUP WHITE VINEGAR

1 CUP RICE WINE VINEGAR

1 Roast the garlic cloves and peppers over an open flame or heat a cast iron skillet and roast until browned.

2 In a high-powered blender, combine the roasted garlic and peppers, water, sugar, and vinegars and puree until smooth.

3 Pour the sauce into a medium saucepan and bring to a boil over medium heat.

4 Reduce the heat and simmer for 20 minutes. Remove from the heat.

5 Transfer the sauce to sterilized bottles when the sauce reaches 180°F. The sauce can be stored in a sealed container for about 6 months.

Serving Tip: Consider straining the sauce through a fine-mesh sieve if you want a thinner sauce.

CHAPTER EIGHT:

Around the World

As we travel around the world exploring hot sauces and salsas, you will have noticed that each region of the world has its own style for making these concoctions. Most sauces created in Africa and Israel are delicious and herbaceous, using fresh cilantro, basil, and finely chopped parsley, mixed with other ingredients. If you're not yet familiar with the wonderful world of African and Middle Eastern sauces, these might remind you of an Argentinean chimichurri. I love these on meats and fish and in stews and falafels. Here are a few recipes that you can make in the comfort of your own home. Enjoy!

MEDITERRANEAN PEPPER SAUCE

Popular in Mediterranean countries such as Greece, this sauce is a great way to spice things up, especially alongside fish or grilled vegetable dishes. For the best flavor, make this ahead of time to allow flavors to meld together.

Makes: about 1 quart
Prep time: 10 minutes

1 (10-OUNCE) JAR OF ROASTED RED PEPPERS, DRAINED

2 GARLIC CLOVES

¼ CUP SLIVERED ALMONDS

1 TEASPOON GROUND CUMIN

½ TEASPOON PAPRIKA

1 TEASPOON RED PEPPER FLAKES

½ TEASPOON SALT

1 TABLESPOON EXTRA-VIRGIN OLIVE OIL

1 TABLESPOON RED WINE VINEGAR

1 In a food processor or high-speed blender, combine the peppers, garlic, almonds, cumin, paprika, red pepper flakes, salt, olive oil, and vinegar and blend until the sauce reaches the desired consistency.

2 Scrape the sauce into a serving dish if you wish to eat immediately, or store in a sealable container in the refrigerator for up to 2 weeks.

Ingredient Tip: Try using smoked paprika to add a smoky flavor to this sauce.

HARISSA

Harissa is a North African hot chile pepper paste. Tunisians use this condiment on most dishes; as a marinade for beef, poultry, goat and lamb; and also on couscous and in soups and stews.

Makes: 1 quart
Prep time: 10 minutes
Cook time:
40 minutes

2 WHOLE RED BELL PEPPERS, HALVED AND SEEDED

8 RED FRESNO PEPPERS, HALVED AND SEEDED

8 WHOLE GARLIC CLOVES, DIVIDED

2 TEASPOONS CUMIN SEEDS

2 TEASPOONS CORIANDER SEEDS

2 TABLESPOONS LEMON JUICE

2 TABLESPOONS TOMATO PASTE

2 TABLESPOONS EXTRA-VIRGIN OLIVE OIL

2 TEASPOONS KOSHER SALT

1 Preheat the oven to 400°F.

2 On a rimmed baking sheet, place the bell peppers, Fresno peppers, and 4 garlic cloves and roast in the oven for 20 minutes, turning once halfway through.

3 Remove the Fresno peppers and garlic from the pan and continue roasting the bell peppers for another 15 minutes. Once the bell peppers are nicely charred, take them out of the oven to cool.

4 While the bell peppers roast, put the cumin and coriander seeds in a dry skillet and toast for 3 minutes, being careful not to burn them. You'll want the seeds to be fragrant.

5 Use a mortar and pestle to grind the seeds into a powder. Reserve.

continued

6 After the Fresno peppers and bell peppers have cooled enough to handle, peel the charred skin from them and roughly chop.

7 Put all the ingredients into a food processor or high-speed blender and run it until you have a paste-like consistency. If you need to smooth the sauce out, add more olive oil little by little until the sauce reaches the desired texture.

8 Transfer to a sealable container and enjoy immediately or store in the refrigerator for up to 2 weeks.

Substitution Tip: If you can't find red Fresno chiles, substitute red jalapeños.

Ingredient Tip: Add reconstituted dried chipotle peppers for a smoky flavor. To reconstitute a dried pepper, simply add it to a small pot of boiling water for 8 minutes or until ready.

ISRAELI HOT SAUCE

This recipe is used by many Israelis for just about every dish they make. Shawarma, spicy eggplant, flatbreads, hummus, and rice dishes are some favorites to use this sauce on. If you're unfamiliar with it, it might remind you of chimichurri, but this sauce is spicier.

Makes: about 1½ quarts
Prep time: 10 minutes

3 BUNCHES FRESH CILANTRO

4 TABLESPOONS FRESHLY SQUEEZED LIME JUICE

½ CUP EXTRA-VIRGIN OLIVE OIL

5 GARLIC CLOVES, MINCED

8 RED THAI PEPPERS

1 TEASPOON GROUND CUMIN

1 TEASPOON GROUND CARDAMOM

1 TEASPOON FRESHLY GROUND BLACK PEPPER

SALT

1 In a high-speed blender, combine the cilantro, lime juice, and oil in a blender and process until you have a paste-like consistency.

2 Add the garlic, chiles, cumin, cardamom, and black pepper and puree until smooth. Add salt to taste.

3 Store in a sealed container for 2 to 3 weeks or in the freezer for 6 months.

SHATTA

If you haven't encountered shatta before, it might remind you of a spicy pesto sauce. It is used throughout the Middle East and is really amazing on the Egyptian dish kushari. I really enjoy this on my beans or drizzled into hummus.

Makes: about 1 pint
Prep time: 10 minutes

1 BUNCH FRESH CILANTRO
1 BUNCH FRESH PARSLEY
2 GARLIC CLOVES
6 GREEN JALAPEÑO PEPPERS, CHOPPED
1 AFRICAN BIRD'S EYE PEPPER
1 TABLESPOON KOSHER SALT
1 TEASPOON GROUND CUMIN
1 TABLESPOON FRESHLY GROUND BLACK PEPPER
½ CUP EXTRA-VIRGIN OLIVE OIL
2 TABLESPOONS WHITE WINE VINEGAR

1 In a high-speed blender, combine all the ingredients and puree until the sauce reaches a fine, salsa-like consistency.

2 Transfer the sauce to a bowl and enjoy, or transfer to a sealable container and store in the refrigerator for up to 2 weeks.

Ingredient Tip: Use water or more oil to help puree the sauce if necessary.

NIGERIAN PEPPER SAUCE

A great sauce to use on fried beef and peppered meats. This is also delicious on jollof rice and many meat stews.

Makes: about 1 quart
Prep time: 15 minutes
Cook time: 1 hour and 5 minutes

2 LARGE RED BELL PEPPERS, SEEDED AND CHOPPED

20 RED THAI PEPPERS OR RED SERRANO PEPPERS, CHOPPED

2 HABANERO PEPPERS, CHOPPED

1 LARGE RED ONION, CHOPPED

2 CUPS VEGETABLE OIL

2 TABLESPOONS BOUILLON POWDER

SALT

1 In a high-speed blender, combine the bell peppers, chiles, habanero peppers, and onion and puree.

2 Strain the mixture through a fine-mesh sieve, reserving the solids. Discard the liquids.

3 In a large saucepan, heat the vegetable oil over medium-high heat for approximately 1 minute, or until hot.

4 Fry the pepper solids for 3 minutes; then stir in the bouillon powder.

5 Loosely cover the pan and simmer for 1 hour, stirring frequently so as not to burn the sauce. Add salt to taste.

6 Cool, bottle, and store the sauce in a sealed container in the refrigerator for up to 2 weeks.

AFRICAN PEPPER SAUCE

This West African recipe is great on rice dishes, chicken, and curry. It's very spicy! Proceed with caution!

Makes: 1 quart
Prep time: 10 minutes
Cook time:
25 minutes

4 MEDIUM YELLOW ONIONS, QUARTERED

2 TOMATOES, QUARTERED

⅓ CUP GROUND GINGER

5 SCOTCH BONNET OR HABANERO PEPPERS

1 GARLIC CLOVE

½ CUP VEGETABLE OIL

1 TABLESPOON CHICKEN BOUILLON

1 TEASPOON SALT

1 In a high-speed blender, combine the onion, tomatoes, ginger, peppers, and garlic and puree.

2 In a large saucepan, heat the oil over medium heat and add the puree, bouillon, and salt. Stir to combine.

3 Sauté for 25 minutes, stirring occasionally.

4 Cool and bottle the sauce or store in the refrigerator for up to 3 weeks (or freeze for future use).

Ingredient Tip: Cilantro works really well in this. Add 1 cup of fresh cilantro during step 1 to taste.

PERI-PERI SAUCE

This is an African spicy sauce made with the infamous bird's eye chile. One of the most popular sauces in Africa, there are several variations of this sauce. Here is the most common way to prepare the infamous African Peri-Peri sauce.

Makes: 1⅓ cups
Prep time: 15 minutes

¾ POUND AFRICAN BIRD'S EYE PEPPERS

5 GARLIC CLOVES

1 TEASPOON SMOKED PAPRIKA

⅓ CUP FRESH CILANTRO

¼ CUP CHOPPED FRESH BASIL

½ CUP EXTRA-VIRGIN OLIVE OIL

JUICE OF 1 LEMON

KOSHER SALT

1   In a high-speed blender, combine the peppers, garlic, paprika, cilantro, basil, oil, and lemon juice.

2   Blend to the desired consistency, but this is usually served smooth. Add salt to taste. Transfer to a sealable container and store in the refrigerator for up to 2 weeks.

Substitution Tip: Substitute red chiles if bird's eye peppers are not available.

WEST AFRICAN PEPPER SAUCE

This is very similar to the African Pepper Sauce (page 104), but with a twist. The difference is the use of parsley and basil, which give the sauce a fresher taste.

Makes: about 1 quart
Prep time: 10 minutes
Cook time: 15 minutes

6 HABANERO OR SCOTCH BONNET PEPPERS

1 SMALL WHITE ONION, ROUGHLY CHOPPED

5 GARLIC CLOVES

2 WHOLE FRESH BASIL LEAVES

2 TABLESPOONS ROUGHLY CHOPPED FRESH PARSLEY

3 MEDIUM TOMATOES, ROUGHLY CHOPPED

¾ CUP EXTRA-VIRGIN OLIVE OIL

KOSHER SALT

FRESHLY GROUND BLACK PEPPER

1 In a high-speed blender or food processor, combine the peppers, onion, garlic, basil, parsley, tomatoes, and oil and blend until smooth.

2 Transfer the mixture to a large saucepan.

3 Bring to a boil over medium-high heat, stirring constantly.

4 Season with salt and fresh pepper to taste.

5 Cool, bottle in sterilized containers, and store in the refrigerator for up to 1 month.

Ingredient Tip: Add more peppers for an even spicier sauce! Be warned, however—this one's already pretty hot.

CHAPTER NINE:

Other Hot Sauces

I love to cook! Most of the sauces I create are based on the meals I prepare. Although it's easier to buy a jarred marinade or sauce when a recipe calls for it, I like to make my own. That way I know I am using the freshest, most natural ingredients without preservatives. Besides, making your own sauce only takes a few minutes longer. In this final chapter, I will share a few of my favorite sauce recipes that I use when cooking.

CRANBERRY-JALAPEÑO GLAZE

This spicy glaze is wonderful for toast and even on peanut butter and jelly sandwiches. I also like to slather some on my chicken or ribs in the last 10 minutes of grilling. It caramelizes so well!

Makes: about 1 quart
Prep time: 15 minutes
Cook time: 10 minutes, plus 24 hours of rest time

2 CUPS FRESH CRANBERRIES (CAN SUBSTITUTE FROZEN)
1 CUP WATER
2 CUPS JALAPEÑO PEPPERS, STEMMED AND SEEDED
2 CUPS APPLE CIDER VINEGAR
5½ CUPS WHITE SUGAR
2 PACKETS LIQUID PECTIN

1   In a high-speed blender, combine the cranberries, water, jalapeños, and vinegar and puree.

2   Transfer the mixture to a large pot, add the sugar and pectin, and bring to a boil. Simmer for 3 minutes

3   Let the glaze cool to 180°F and fill 9 or 10 sterilized 8-ounce jars.

4   Let stand for 24 hours and store in the refrigerator for up to 1 year.

Ingredient Tip: Add a habanero for more heat.

SPICY NASHVILLE HOT SAUCE

This sauce recipe is used for a marinade when making Nashville chicken sandwiches or when eating chicken prepared in any way. I call it my go-to "chicken sauce."

Makes: 1 pint
Prep time: 5 minutes
Cook time: 5 minutes

½ CUP UNSALTED BUTTER

3 TABLESPOONS GROUND CAYENNE

2 TABLESPOONS BROWN SUGAR

2 TEASPOONS SALT

3 TEASPOONS FRESHLY GROUND BLACK PEPPER

2 TEASPOONS GARLIC POWDER

1 TEASPOON SMOKED PAPRIKA

1 TABLESPOONS HONEY

1 In a medium saucepan, combine all the ingredients and stir over low heat.

2 Simmer for 3 minutes.

3 Remove the sauce from the heat and transfer to sealable containers. Store in the refrigerator for up to 2 weeks.

Ingredient Tip: Use a dash of vinegar for a more tart flavor.

SPICY RED ENCHILADA SAUCE

I consider this another Mikey V's staple when making enchiladas. I also use this sauce as a base for any Mexican-style soups like menudo or pozole.

Makes: about
1½ pints
Prep time: 10 minutes,
plus 20 minutes
soaking time
Cook time:
30 minutes

4 DRIED CHILE DE ARBOL PEPPERS

5 DRIED GUAJILLO PEPPERS

5 DRIED ANCHO PEPPERS

1 TABLESPOON VEGETABLE OIL

1 SMALL YELLOW ONION, CHOPPED

4 CLOVES GARLIC, MINCED

1 CUP CHICKEN OR BEEF BROTH

FRESHLY GROUND BLACK PEPPER

1 In a medium skillet over medium heat, toast the dried chile de arbol, guajillo, and ancho chile peppers.

2 Set the chiles in a bowl of hot water to soak for about 20 minutes. Reserve a small amount of the soaking water.

3 Move the chiles to a high-speed blender and puree with a bit of the reserve water.

4 In same skillet, combine the vegetable oil, onion, and garlic and sauté until they become translucent.

5 Let the onion mixture cool and add it to the chiles in the blender.

6 Add the broth to blender and puree until you reach desired consistency. Use additional reserve water if necessary. Add salt and pepper to taste.

7 Transfer the sauce to sealable containers and store in the refrigerator for up to 2 weeks.

FERMENTED GARLIC AND SERRANO HOT SAUCE

Using fermented serrano peppers, this tasty sauce can be used to spice up and accompany any dish you prepare! This one takes a bit longer but is definitely worth the wait.

Makes: about 1 quart
Prep time: 20 minutes
Cook time: 20 minutes
Ferment time: 7 to 14 days

1 POUND SERRANO PEPPERS

4 GARLIC CLOVES, MINCED

4 CUPS WATER

1/2 CUP WHITE WINE VINEGAR

1 OUNCE TEQUILA

3 TABLESPOONS KOSHER SALT

JUICE OF 1 LIME

1   To ferment the serrano peppers, put them in a high-speed blender with garlic and puree. Pack them into a large jar, leaving 1 inch of headspace.

2   Mix water, vinegar, tequila, and salt and pour enough over peppers to cover. Save any remaining brine for later use. Keep the peppers covered in brine! Screw on the lid and store in a cool, dark place, such as your pantry.

3   Check the mixture daily to make sure the peppers remain covered in brine. Burp the jars often by unscrewing the jars and releasing the accumulated gases. Do this for 1 to 2 weeks.

4   Pour the fermented peppers and their brine into a large saucepan and bring to a boil. Simmer for 15 minutes.

5   Let the sauce cool slightly; then transfer it to the blender and puree.

6   Add a splash of lime juice, strain through a fine-mesh sieve, and pour into sterilized bottles. Store in the refrigerator for up to 1 year.

FIERY FERMENTED HOT SAUCE

This is a quick fermented recipe that takes about 5 days to finish. The longer you let this ferment, the better the sauce tastes.

Makes: about 1 quart
Prep time: 15 minutes
Cook time:
30 minutes, plus
45 minutes rest time
Ferment time:
5 to 7 days

2 DRIED CHILE DE ARBOL PEPPERS

2 DRIED GUAJILLO PEPPERS

2 CUPS CHOPPED SERRANO PEPPERS

1 RED BELL PEPPER, SEEDED AND CHOPPED

1 SMALL WHITE ONION, CHOPPED

6 GARLIC CLOVES

1 TABLESPOON KOSHER SALT

1½ CUPS WHITE VINEGAR

1 In a medium skillet, toast the dried chile de arbol and guajillo peppers over medium-high heat. Do not overtoast them, as they will taste rancid.

2 Combine the toasted peppers with the serranos, bell pepper, onion, garlic, salt, and vinegar in a large mixing bowl and let stand for 45 minutes.

3 Transfer the mixture to a high-speed blender and puree until the desired consistency is reached.

4 Pour the mixture into sterilized canning jars, cover with cheesecloth, and secure it with rubber bands.

5 Let the jars stand in a cool, dark place for 5 days.

6 Seal each jar with a lid and refrigerate for up to 3 months.

Recipe Tip: The longer you let this sauce sit, the deeper and more flavorful it becomes.

ROASTED GARLIC AND GHOST PEPPER SAUCE

Ghost peppers typically have a smoky flavor already, but with this recipe you'll get smoky and roasted flavors from all the ingredients!

Makes: about 1 quart
Prep time: 10 minutes
Cook time:
20 minutes

4 FRESH GHOST PEPPERS, CHOPPED

5 GARLIC CLOVES

1 MEDIUM CARROT, CHOPPED

¼ CUP APPLE CIDER VINEGAR

JUICE OF 1 LEMON

1 TABLESPOON SALT

½ CUP WATER

1 Preheat the oven to 375°F, turn on a fan, and open all the windows!

2 Place the ghost peppers, garlic, and carrot on a baking sheet.

3 Roast for 15 to 20 minutes, or until softened

4 Add the roasted peppers, garlic, carrot, vinegar, lemon juice, and salt to a high-speed blender.

5 Puree until smooth, adding water 1 teaspoon at a time until the sauce reaches the desired consistency.

6 Bottle the sauce and store in the refrigerator for up to 4 weeks.

Ingredient Tip: You may use dried (reconstituted) ghost peppers if fresh peppers are not available. Add dried peppers to a small pan of boiling water to reconstitute.

YELLOW FATALII HOT SAUCE

The yellow fatalii pepper is one of my favorite peppers to work with. It has a floral flavor with a habanero-style burn that is intense. Great on all Caribbean- and Mexican-style foods.

Makes: about 1 quart
Prep time: 20 minutes
Cook time:
20 minutes

10 YELLOW FATALII PEPPERS

1 MEDIUM CARROT, PEELED AND CHOPPED

½ LARGE WHITE ONION, CHOPPED

4 GARLIC CLOVES

1 TABLESPOON HONEY

1 TABLESPOON GROUND GINGER

1 TABLESPOON GROUND MUSTARD

1 TABLESPOON GROUND TURMERIC

1 TEASPOON KOSHER SALT

1 TEASPOON WHITE PEPPER

½ CUP APPLE CIDER VINEGAR

½ CUP WATER

1   Add the peppers, carrot, onion, garlic, honey, ginger, mustard, turmeric, salt, pepper, and vinegar to a large pot and bring to a boil, stirring occasionally. Reduce the heat and simmer for 15 minutes.

2   Pour the mixture into a food processor and blend until smooth. Add water 1 teaspoon at a time if you prefer a thinner sauce.

3   Bottle and refrigerate for up to 3 weeks.

Substitution Tip: This recipe works well with any kind of chile pepper in place of the yellow fataliis. Use a milder pepper for a milder sauce. Use a spicier pepper for a sauce that's even hotter than this one!

GREEN GHOST PEPPER SAUCE

This is a family favorite of mine using ghost peppers. If you don't like it so hot, omit the ghost peppers and use jalapeños.

Makes: about 1 quart
Prep time: 10 minutes

1 BUNCH OF CILANTRO LEAVES

2 FRESH GHOST PEPPERS, ROUGHLY CHOPPED

2 JALAPEÑO PEPPERS, STEMMED AND CHOPPED

6 TABLESPOONS SOUR CREAM

3 TABLESPOONS MAYONNAISE

JUICE OF ½ LIME

3 CLOVES GARLIC, MINCED

DRIZZLE OF EXTRA-VIRGIN OLIVE OIL

SALT

FRESHLY GROUND BLACK PEPPER

1 In a food processor or high-speed blender, combine the cilantro, peppers, sour cream, mayonnaise, lime juice, garlic, and olive oil and blend until smooth.

2 Add salt and pepper to taste.

3 Bottle the sauce and refrigerate for up to 3 weeks.

Storage Tip: Mix well before serving.

SRIRACHA-SCORPION HOT SAUCE

This super-hot Scorpion pepper sauce is a delicious combination of jalapeños and Scorpion peppers to use on eggs and tacos. When tasting this sauce, you will get the sweetness from the sriracha sauce first. Shortly after that, the scorpion peppers will sting your taste buds!

Makes: about 1 pint
Prep time: 15 minutes
Cook time:
20 minutes

1 CUP RED JALAPEÑO PEPPERS, CHOPPED

2 SCORPION PEPPERS, HALVED

2 TABLESPOONS WHITE VINEGAR

1 TABLESPOON APPLE CIDER VINEGAR

5 GARLIC CLOVES

1 TABLESPOON SALT

4 TEASPOONS SUGAR

1   Add all the ingredients to a high-speed blender and puree.

2   Transfer the mixture to a small saucepan and simmer for 15 minutes.

3   Let cool and puree again, adding water if needed to reach the desired consistency.

4   Bottle the sauce in sterilized containers and refrigerate for up to 4 weeks.

CILANTRO-REAPER HOT SAUCE

This is a chile-head's dream! If your mouth is broken and you can't get enough of a super-hot sauce in your life, then this is the recipe for you. This recipe is not for the average person. You must be an experienced chile-head to try it. Please use caution with this bad boy!

Makes: about 1 quart
Prep time: 15 minutes
Cook time:
30 minutes

15 TO 20 DEHYDRATED CAROLINA REAPER PEPPERS

1½ CUPS WHITE VINEGAR

1 CUP ROUGHLY CHOPPED FRESH CILANTRO

½ CUP FRESHLY SQUEEZED LEMON JUICE

½ CUP FRESHLY SQUEEZED LIME JUICE

2 TABLESPOONS SUGAR

3 GARLIC CLOVES

½ SMALL YELLOW ONION, CHOPPED

1 TABLESPOON KOSHER SALT, PLUS MORE TO TASTE

1   Soak the dehydrated peppers for 5 minutes in hot water until softened. Drain water.

2   In a high-speed blender, combine all the ingredients and process until smooth.

3   Transfer the mixture to a medium pot and bring to a boil. Simmer for 25 minutes.

4   Remove from the heat and let cool.

5   Season to taste with additional salt.

6   Transfer the sauce to sterilized bottles when it is at least 180°F and refrigerate for up to 3 months.

Recipe Tip: Make sure to open all windows and turn on all fans before attempting to cook this recipe. Always use gloves and eye protection when handling hot peppers.

measurement conversions

Volume Equivalents (Dry)

US STANDARD	METRIC (APPROX.)
⅛ teaspoon	0.5 mL
¼ teaspoon	1 mL
½ teaspoon	2 mL
¾ teaspoon	4 mL
1 teaspoon	5 mL
1 tablespoon	15 mL
¼ cup	59 mL
⅓ cup	79 mL
½ cup	118 mL
⅔ cup	156 mL
¾ cup	177 mL
1 cup	235 mL
2 cups or 1 pint	475 mL
3 cups	700 mL
4 cups or 1 quart	1 L
½ gallon	2 L
1 gallon	4 L

Volume Equivalents (Liquid)

US STANDARD	US STANDARD (OUNCES)	METRIC (APPROX.)
2 tablespoons	1 fl. oz.	30 mL
¼ cup	2 fl. oz.	60 mL
½ cup	4 fl. oz.	120 mL
1 cup	8 fl. oz.	240 mL
1½ cups	12 fl. oz.	355 mL
2 cups or 1 pint	16 fl. oz.	475 mL
4 cups or 1 quart	32 fl. oz.	1 L
1 gallon	128 fl. oz.	4 L

Oven Temperatures

FAHRENHEIT (F)	CELSIUS (C) (APPROX.)
250°F	120°C
300°F	150°C
325°F	165°C
350°F	180°C
375°F	190°C
400°F	200°C
425°F	220°C
450°F	230°C

appendix:
starting your own hot sauce business

You've finally perfected your own hot sauce; now what? That's right, it's time to get it on the market! There are several things you must know before you take that next step. Do you need a license? Can you legally make it in your own kitchen? Do you have to have your sauce tested? Who do you send it to for shelf-life testing? You may have asked yourself one or all these questions in the past. There is one simple answer: do your research, have a plan, and then execute!

Disclaimer: It is a good idea to find out your local rules and regulations regarding food processing before you start your business venture. It is unsafe and illegal to sell unlicensed processed foods.

* Have a great recipe that has been replicated several times. Have your friends and family taste-test it for you. Send it to hot sauce reviewers and ask them for their honest opinions.
* Create your business profile. Will you be a sole proprietor, partnership, LLC, or corporation?

- Register for federal business licensing with the IRS.
- Send your finished product to a process authority for testing and process review. Most universities have a process authority on site and offer shelf-life testing for a reasonable fee.
- Find a place to process. You can process yourself in a commercial kitchen that you rent or find a co-packer that will process your sauce for you and save you time. This works especially well if you have a full-time job and do not have the time to spend hours in the kitchen packaging things yourself. Remember to sign a nondisclosure agreement before entering into a contract. This is done to protect you so that nobody can steal your recipe and use it as their own.
- Start working on a logo and label for your brand.
- Get a nutritional panel created for your product.
- Label requirements: Consult with your state inspector about what is required for your state. Most states follow basic FDA regulations, but there are some states that require state-specific items (such as font sizes for the logo, placements of nutritional panel and ingredient statements, etc.) and require certain contact info.
- Get business insurance. Most festivals and farmers' markets require proof of business insurance. Shop around and ask other people in the industry for recommendations.
- Now you're ready to print some labels, make some sauce, and sell, sell, sell!

resources

PepperFool.com

PepperFool.com is a blog full of recipes and tricks when it comes to cooking.

TheHotPepper.com

This website is full of information on everything spicy. If you're looking to grow hot peppers, make a hot sauce, or source some spicy powders, TheHotPepper.com is your place.

ChiliPepperMadness.com

Mike, an avid cook and chili-head, started this website several years ago to appease the spicy food lover's addiction. The website has hundreds of recipes, along with tips on how to preserve and grow chili pepper plants.

Tabasco.com

Today's most iconic and well-known sauces, Tabasco.com tells the story of how it pioneered the hot sauce industry. Over 100 years later, Tabasco is still a thriving company, and you can order many of its products from their site. You can also order collectibles and other memorabilia or check out a recipe or two.

references

Anonymous. "About the Hot Sauce Festival." *Austin Chronicle*. Accessed July 2, 2020. austinchronicle.com/hot-sauce/about.

Anonymous. "The History of Tabasco Brand." Accessed July 2, 2020. tabasco.com/tabasco-history.

Greenaway, Twilight. "How Hot Is That Pepper? How Scientists Measure Spiciness." January 10, 2013. *Smithsonian Magazine*. smithsonianmag.com/arts-culture/how-hot-is-that-pepper-how-scientists-measure-spiciness-884380.

Seitz-Wald, Alex. "Actually, Salsa Dethroned Ketchup 20 Years Ago." *The Atlantic*. October 17, 2013. theatlantic.com/national/archive/2013/10/actually-salsa-dethroned-ketchup-20-years-ago/309844.

index

acknowledgments

I'd like to thank my wife, Tanya, for not only being my partner in life but helping me with the wording and grammar in this book. Thank you for continuing to push me in everything I do. I love you.

To all the pioneers in the hot sauce industry, thanks a million! Companies like Tabasco, Sriracha, Cholula, and Tapatío: You've helped keep the industry striving for years.

Thanks to a personal industry mentor of mine, John Hard. Thanks for paving the way for sauce companies like mine, for motivating me to become a better saucemaker, and for teaching me to settle for nothing less than becoming number one in the industry.

Thanks to Hot Licks in Seaport Village, San Diego, for introducing me to the world of craft hot sauces while growing up, especially Ring of Fire.

Finally, a gigantic thanks to all Mikey V's Foods and spicy food lovers around the world. Without you I wouldn't be able to create these flavorful sauces for you to enjoy!

Keep it spicy!

about the author

Award-winning hot sauce maker Mikey V. has been manufacturing his products professionally since 2012. He began marketing his brand at local street fairs after his Original Red Salsa won first place at the 2012 *Austin Chronicle* Hot Sauce Festival. Mikey added more sauces to his brand, and in March 2015 he opened Mikey V's Hot Sauce Shop in the historic downtown Georgetown Square in Georgetown, Texas. This veteran (USMC) hot sauce manufacturer/co-packer offers an array of products that include hot sauces, salsas, beef jerky, spicy pickles, BBQ sauces, dip mixes, and seasonings. He travels the country to participate in various hot sauce festivals and continues to win awards.

CPSIA information can be obtained
at www.ICGtesting.com
Printed in the USA
BVHW092355251020
591713BV00005B/5

9 781647 391362